Seared With Ink

Portraits of Life in Poetry and Prose

BY: S. J. FERRANDI

SEARED WITH INK

Portraits of Life in Poetry and Prose

SILVER POND PRESS

An imprint of:

Argenti MEDIA, LLC

8775 Centre Park Drive, Suite 452
Columbia, Maryland 21045
443-957-4555 * ArgentiMedia.com

Seared with Ink – Portraits of Life in Poetry and Prose

A collection of poems and prose by
S.J. Ferrandi
original artwork
by the Craigslist Artists Project

Cover and Book Design by Lori J. Sublett

First Edition

ISBN – 10   0615326633
ISBN – 13   9780615326634

Library of Congress Cataloging-in Publication Data
Ferrandi, S.J. ,1964-
Seared with Ink: Portraits of Life in Poetry and Prose

This book printed in China

Seared with Ink

Portraits of Life in Poetry and Prose

Dedicated to Jacob & Julian

Seared with Ink
Portraits of Life in Poetry and Prose

In appreciation

Harry Chapin, the first person who showed me the power of a story with his songs. I spent my teenage years listening every night in the darkness of my bedroom to his words as those marvelous story songs came alive in the theater of my mind. He showed me with well chosen words, it was possible to tell a beautiful story of a life rich in complexity contained on a single page.

Dedication

To the women who supported my words with their critiques and compliments:

Lisa Ferrandi, she has listened to me even when the words weren't so poetic. She has walked with me on my journey through this life in darkness and light and has given me my greatest gift, my sons, Jacob and Julian.

Virginia Ferrandi, my mother, who always loved my words and supported me with hers.

George, my sister, the brilliant artist, who challenges me with her thoughts and is still the finest writer I've ever known. Thanks for always pushing me to go further down the path on my journey with words.

Clarinda Harris, a wonderful poet and friend, my first poetry teacher, who after 25 years is still there to question a word or give me praise; my fan.

Kate Mirabile, my sister, separated at birth, I'm sure, and raised by parents just like mine. It was she who convinced me to write more and share my words in this book. I found my words, while she found her innerjock; the two of us sharing our midlife crisis by doing what we didn't believe was possible.

Lori Sublett and Erin Fiato, two great friends, who make me laugh everyday and never let me get too full of myself even when I think I'm still the boss. Thanks for always being there when I need you and listening to these poems more times than you really wanted to.

Carol Mox, my friend and proofreader, who always knows her way around my words even when I don't know myself. Thanks for always being there with your red pen and a box of extra commas.

Kelly Shinnick, another good friend, who freely shared her artistic vision for this book as well as six inspiring paintings. She is a wickedly funny woman who brings out the humor in any room.

Maureeen Nicholas, Kate Jordan, Shamira Diggs, Barbara Lawson and Michele Kornbluth who shared their insight, guidance and wisdom with me as we read these poems together.

SEARED WITH INK

Portraits of Life in Poetry and Prose

INDEX OF POEMS

SEARED WITH INK

Portraits of Life in Poetry and Prose

THE HISTORY OF THE CRAIGSLIST ARTIST PROJECT

What would happen if complete strangers, several dozen of them, had the opportunity to read and create beautiful art around my words? That was the crazy idea I had while stuck in traffic in the spring of 2009. Rather than just have Lori Sublett, a dear friend and a talented artist, or my sister George, the most creative person I know, who happens to be a well respected, professional artist illustrate my artwork, what if I asked complete strangers who answered an online ad on Craigslist do it. What would the results be?

Spectacular.

This book, all of the words by me, and all of the beautiful artwork by talented artists, most of whom I have never met came together over the internet during the summer of 2009. The goal in creating this book was simple; let the words of my stories convey a message that would reach the creative spirit of many different artists and let the beauty of their work accompany my words.

This was a collaborative project in the truest sense of the word. I hope you enjoy my poetry and prose and see in the portraits of the many people whose lives are lived entirely in these poems as friends and strangers that you already know.

I thank you for reading my words and appreciating the beautiful works of art that accompany them. Sometimes a crazy idea can be a powerful, beautiful expression in itself.

S.J. Ferrandi

Seared with Ink
Portraits of Life in Poetry and Prose

Index of Artists

POEMS

In the darkness at five each morning
they come to me
dropped off
by the tooth fairy
or the angel of mercy
on their way back to the heavens.
Words
gift wrapped like lovers' chocolates
or
left
in a rotting heap
in the corner of the room
for me to mop up
and
ferment
into a bitter elixir
to be imbibed
slowly
by adults
after signing a release form
acknowledging the danger of their consumption.

11 February 2009

MAKING PEOPLE THINK

Virgin pulp rushing down rolling presses
seared with ink
spilling words upon the page
making people think.

Writer's joys found lost upon the shelves
of some prestigious university
consuming space
dedicated by one Morris Q. Racceloff
in memory of his mother.

Wrinkled hands beyond the ivy walls
protesting the ideas of men lost from God
banning words from hungry hearts
of impressionable youth.

Poet proud
(and just as poor)
to think that I made someone think.

13 January 1985

Dinner argument encouraged breakfast in bed

Love

Thursdays at Two

I still have that business card, now faded and gray,
that you handed me at our first meeting.
I was a young woman who had been left the family farm
and wanted to invest for the future, my future.
Trapped within a marriage arranged by my father
to a man I did not love and could not leave
with three children at my knee
and another on the way.

                                        You were, as I had been told by my father's lawyer,
                                                   young and handsome,
                   with a whisper of gray that made you even more distinguished,
                                   in your three piece herringbone suit

I took a taxi into the city
and an elevator up to your skyscraper office.
Your secretary offered me tea,
while I fiddled with my plastic pearls.
Nervous, and unsure, I wore the gingham dress
I bought earlier that spring
for Easter dinner at my mother-in-law's.

                                                        with a checkered bowtie,
                                              than a movie star.

As I sat and explained my dilemma,
you listened intensely.
You talked with me,
not to me or at me, but with me,
in an age when being a woman came with its own curse
that caused men in three piece suits to issue a quick order
and dismiss the woman before they missed their tee time.

You invited me to meet with you each March, June and December
to learn about my investments in railroads and meatpackers,
airlines and gas companies. You sat with me at my side and taught me
how to read the business section of the Sunday newspaper.
From your kindness, our friendship blossomed into love.
Not infatuation or lust, but a bond so strong in friendship, that love is born.

Over the next thirty nine years,
we met in small hideaway restaurants each Thursday at two,
and there we lived the lives of the other.
You watched my children grow in snap shots and stories,
laugher and tears. You cared for me when he hit me
after he lost his job at the plant,
and when my only boy was sent off to war never to come back.
Over coffee, we talked about cancer, dying and that mole on your back
that changed colors and made you think of your father's early death.
You helped me bury my husband,
who died after decades of three packs a day
and fifth of corn whiskey.
I learned about your world of stamps, your dogs and your mother.

Over the years,
you entrusted with me the secret of your big lie,
and told me stories of your boyfriends and one night stands,
married men that you met in private bars or referred by friends.

Once, on my birthday,
after too much wine,
you tried to make love to me, but drunk
and inexperienced,
we spent the afternoon
cuddling on a big king bed
at the fanciest hotel in the city
reserved for Mr. and Mrs. Smith.
You never spoke to me about that day,
nor I to you, but I knew that you deeply loved me,
a girl from a world so far from yours that
you were surprised that I spoke English.

You made sure my investments grew and all my girls went to college.
And I earned your soul and a debt I shall never be able
to repay for you were the truest friend
I have ever had.
Today, holding your hand as you breathed your last breath,
I wiped my tears thinking back to
long ago wearing plastic pearls
and a gingham dress and the future that you gave me.

22 January 2009

13

Morning Prayer

Let me call you beautiful
as the sun rises above your bed
and morning glories unfold
in triumph to the victory of a day
new with endless possibilities.

Let me kiss your lips and make
your dreams come true as the stars
once again play hide-n-seek with
the day bold and bright.

Let me hold you tight as an anchor
in a storm unyielding against waves and rain
as thunder causes men fierce with fight
to whimper at the sound of impending doom.

Let me call you beautiful
and sooth you with wine and verse
as your lips kiss me sweetly
and your arms hold me tight
while darkness gives way to the morning light.

Let me call you beautiful, my beautiful,
and worship you for the rest of my life.

10 July 2009

Stars in Heaven

She's told you she found heaven in your eyes.

I think it's fair to warn you; I think she lies.
She's named a thousand stars that way.
She loves the darkness,
searching for the light,
white, hot, flickering,
in the blackness of it all,
cuz only stars and lonesome lovers
come out at night.
I heard she has a mural
of the constellations
on her bedroom wall
and when it's raining,
she can name them all.

She's told you she found heaven in your eyes.
She told me that too. I think she lies.

11 March 2009

Inspired by Willie Nelson's "She's Not For You"

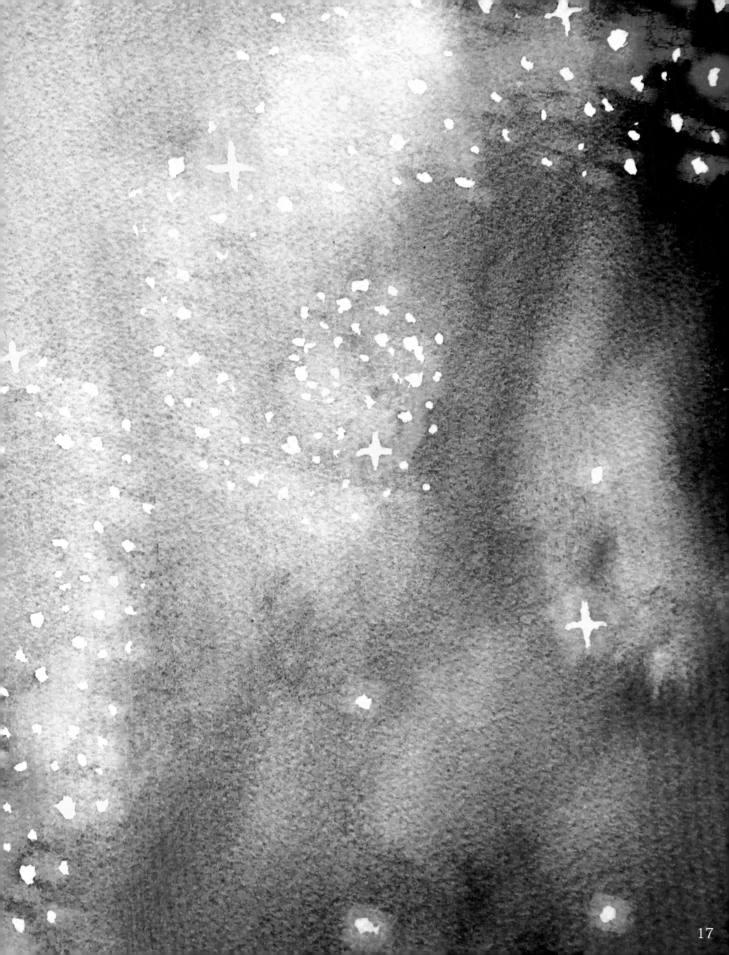

Senior Prom

On a cold day in May,
a sparrow crawled across a rust colored sky
and I knew then that this must be love.
We were grandparents lost from life
by so many days spent mourning our lovers
and our former life of powerbroker and mother,
husband and wife.
I offered an invitation to the theatre
to the sweet lady who shot me a smile each Saturday in shul.
You accepted and finally told me your name.
For the last fifty years I knew you only as
Mrs. Schultze, never Cynthia.

Three months later, laying in bed,
our wrinkled bodies wrapped around one another
filled with passion. Your mouth working me hard until I gasped
as the pain filled my chest,
embarrassed at the thought
that I might cum and go at the same time.
I closed my eyes and enjoyed the ecstasy
that washed over me
and waited for the pain to escape.

She had been so sick for so long and we couldn't and we didn't.
I started to feel my manhood die as I watched her slip from me.
You were blessed, a quick heart attack, and he was gone.
Mine suffered for six years until a stroke finally took her.

Naked and feeling life filling me once again,
I wish I were the same man who fathered five boys,
but all I can do is enjoy this feeling
until at last a few drops are released
and I am seventeen again
at the Senior Prom.

28 October 2008

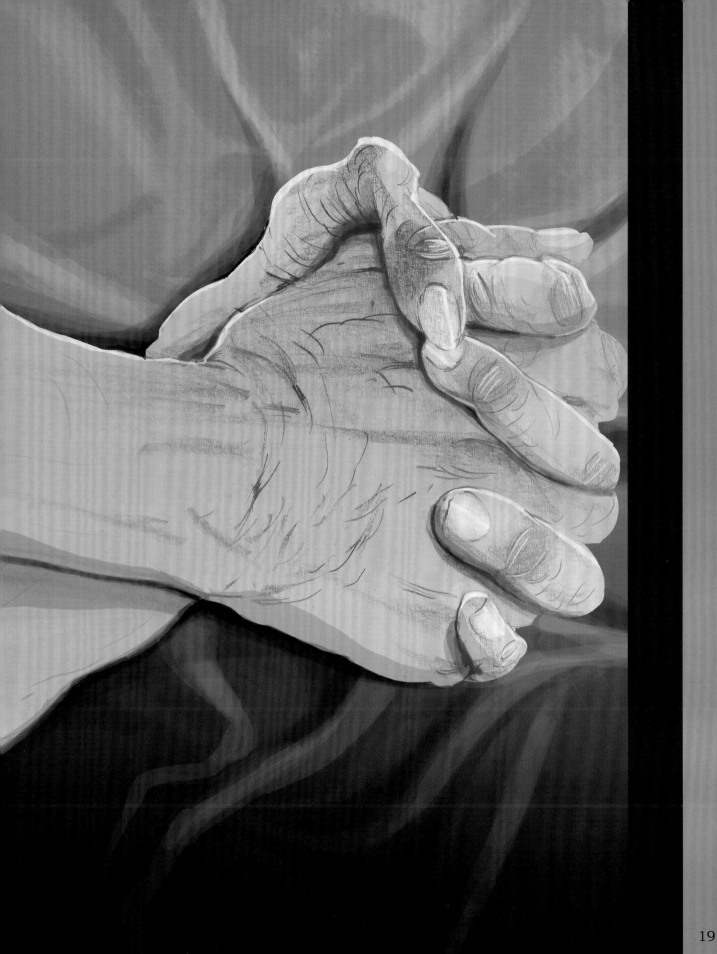

The Wedding Plate

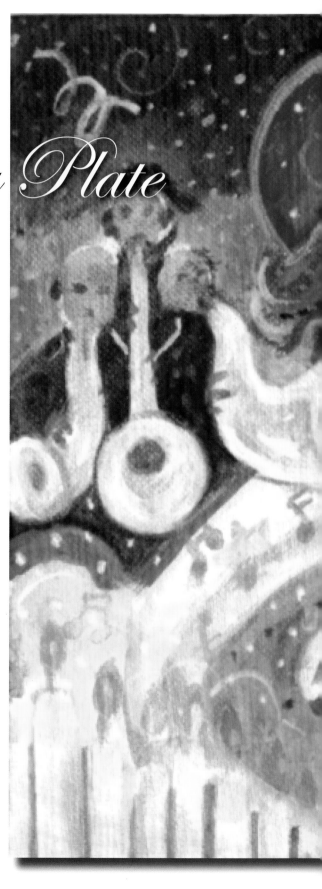

On the plate,
trimmed in green enamel and gold leaf,
lay three pears poached and roasted,
their halves drizzled in a syrup of cognac,
accompanying the braised pork loin,
sliced thin as orchid flowers,
sprinkled with spices from
Argentina that dance on the meat's surface
marrying the flavors of smoke and heat
while five spears of white asparagus
perfumed with a hint of lemon oil
pay homage to the festive meal,
their delicate flavor a
celebration for the gastronome.
The jazz band, imported from Manhattan,
plays in the garden of the historic manor house,
illuminated by a thousand candles glowing,
like votive lights at the Cathedral of the Blessed Mother,
as the couple kiss beneath the stars to the applause
of all their guests.

21 March 2009

A Woman's Prayer

Kiss me in darkness
and let me feel
your hand firmly on my breast

Kiss me in darkness
and let me smell
your scent close to me

Kiss me in darkness
and let me feel
your touch within me

Kiss me in darkness
and let me feel
your hips ride over me

Kiss me in darkness
and let me feel
your sweat fall upon my cheek

Kiss me in darkness
and let your passion
embrace me

Kiss me in darkness
and let me hear
you moan because of me

Kiss me in darkness
and let me take
your breath away

Kiss me in darkness
and fall gently
asleep beside me

26 January 2009

The Art of Making Love

The art of making love begins
with the mind, not the heart,
and never the regions hidden until
darkness to be revealed slowly with
sweet kisses washed with passion
fueled by moonlight.

The art of making love,
beautiful to be remembered on deathbed love,
is more emotional than physical,
and should always be practiced slowly
on a Saturday night after listening to Beethoven
or Miles Davis or the sound of a thousand crickets,
as a banquet of flickering stars shine through the bedroom skylight.

The art of making love, may be completed
under the covers of a warm down comforter
on a snowy Sunday morning at that charming
bed and breakfast in the mountains,
the roads now closed by the storm,
preventing the arrival of guests
and permitting the suspension of time.

The art of making love should always be attempted
gently on rainy Monday mornings, dark for hours more,
the alarm fast asleep, as the sound of rain drops
on windows echoes throughout the room and the pace
of two hearts married for the last forty years
intertwined with that history, quicken at a tender touch.

The art of making love is best on a windy Tuesday,
an hour before sunrise,
on a lost beach, void of vacationers,
a forest of thick reeds swaying in the breeze,
keeping the rhythm as a lone seagull,
a voyeur from the sky, soars overhead.

The art of making love when undertaken on a Wednesday afternoon
should always be proceeded by a bottle of deep red wine
and crusty bread - still warm, served with olive oil and cheese and
foods from the Mediterranean
while gypsy music plays from a neighbor's open window.

The art of making love on a cold Thursday morning
minutes after the postman delivers acceptance letters
to medical school for you both,
should be celebrated loud enough to cause pause
to all who pass by the door of the tiny dorm room
now filled with the sounds of joyous laugher and pure ecstasy.

The art of making love on an oversized sofa
by newlyweds, three days back from their honeymoon,
two weeks of laundry in piles on the floor,
should always begin with
I LOVE YOU as Friday night
slowly fades into Saturday afternoon.

The art of making love should never be attempted by
strangers intoxicated after celebrating St. Patrick's Day
or the wedding of your second cousin, with the person
opposite you becoming more attractive as the fear of returning
home, alone, again,
makes them more beautiful
as you reach for your car keys,
unless you are prepared
to be soul mates
come morning.

22 May 2009

Victory From The Storm

The woman,
in pain,
confused by the storms within her life,
lost from the focus of her world
by the devastating news,
his closet empty, without even a note,
retreats into the solitude
of her home,
alone,
and attempts to nurse her wounds
with a bath,
hot enough to temper
courage and fortitude
from within her meekness.
Afterward, in the darkness of her living room,
lies prostrate, nude,
her body moist and toned and beautiful,
gaining solace in the solitude of the afternoon
as she watches the lightening dance across the summer sky,
its flashes bathing her silhouette in a light of blue,
as the driving summer rain
washes away the girl she use to be
and she rises, after two days in anguish,
a woman with her first victory.

15 April 2009

Scene From an Italian Restaurant

A napkin wet with tears,
Vivaldi played too loudly
for the fine Italian restaurant,
the gray haired waiter,
the father of five daughters,
in the awkward position of serving
the evening's special,
gnocchi with rose cream sauce,
to the beautiful woman in the beaded dress,
distraught,
her boyfriend,
the man of her dreams,
now gone,
after telling her his love for her died
with the abortion.
Gia, the owner's wife, offers to take her upstairs
to their private apartment after pouring a
fine Merlot into the crystal wine glass stained with
crimson lipstick and coaxing her to drink.

1 June 2009

Summer Love

Two silhouettes in the doorway,
illuminated by the flicker of fireflies
and a reading lamp, left on
after her father retired to bed on this hot Friday night,
the sound of crickets thick as the night air.
The form of young lovers undulating
in the darkness, her moan soft as his first caress
until he flicks open both clasps of her bra
releasing her breast, small but firm, to his waiting tongue,
causing her moan to grow deeper as chills of excitement race along
her spine and down to the tips of her fingers pressed hard
against his back.
The metal button of his blue jeans praying
to be unsnapped; a prayer that won't be answered for hours more
as they grope and kiss and fondle
as only young lovers on a hot summer night can do.
At last, the porch illuminated by headlights turning into the driveway
of their historic farmhouse,
her older brother returning home from a date with his new girlfriend,
the scratches along his back covered by his damp sweaty tee shirt.
Silent as he passes the stilled shadows in front of the half opened screen door,
and mercifully turns off that reading lamp
before climbing the stairs to bed.

29 June 2009

Kisses

Your lips,
firm and moist and beautiful,
whisper in the darkness
secrets that make my heart race
as I dream of sunsets at the shore,
holding your hand forty years from now.

Your lips
have kissed me with every type of kiss,
the peck from our first date
gently parted on my cheek
with just enough feeling to let me know I should ask you out again.

The deep passionate kiss of two young lovers
on that spring day by the pond at your grandmother's house,
dragonflies whirling above us as we fell in love
next to your picnic lunch of pulled chicken and dandelion salad.

Your lips,
puckered tight for that kiss, that evolved into wet and memorable,
after I asked your Daddy for your hand,
with my grandmother's ring in mine,
on your birthday, the year you turned nineteen.

There is my favorite kiss;
the one on our wedding day in front of the preacher,
filled with love so deep it reached my soul,
as the choir, singing alleluia,
was drowned out by the applause from all our all our friends.
I opened my eyes to see tears of happiness in yours.

You, twenty hours in labor,
as hard as any day our grandfathers spent
working in the Kentucky coal mines,
looked up at me the night our boy was born,
and gave me a kiss, soft and gentle,
to mark the moment we became a family,
our baby suckling at your breast.

I will always remember the kiss that told me "I'm sorry."
Impatient to go shopping on a night I returned from a week on the road,
dog tired and unwilling to travel thirty miles to the mall,
you lost my wallet filled with Christmas money
from working twenty weeks of overtime,
and us having three boys expecting presents and nothing more to give.

You held my hand tight
and gave me a kiss the day my father died,
that was stronger than any word and washed comfort over me,
on a day I felt like a boy again,
lost at the county fair.

My body covered with your kisses
that made me laugh with delight
as both of us, drunk from fruity drinks, danced nude
around the vacation bed on that island paradise.
We found romance in the darkness
that made our neighbors think we were honeymooners
on our wedding night as they gossiped about us at breakfast.

There were kisses before our boys came back from Scout trips on lazy Sunday
mornings, long and luscious kisses in the darkness before sunrise.
And make up kisses before we went to bed,
angry at a fault or shortcoming
that let me know time would heal that wound.

You held my face with both hands
as you kissed me slowly on Monday mornings,
my truck warming up before
I'd drive across five states
with a load of apples
or orders to deliver rolls of steel
to a factory in the Midwest.
The time away from you,
a sacrifice made, since the plant closed,
September, seven years ago.

I was in Iowa when I got the dreadful news,
about the car accident that brought you here.
I bobtailed back fast,
my Katie in a coma.
My rig a blur across America
as tears streamed down my face,
thinking the worst, as I flew along that interstate.

Your face swollen
and your mouth filled with tubes that keep you alive.
The doctors tell me there is nothing they can do
as I watch the green line race
in even patterns of triangles
across the monitor.
Your eyes are fixed, seeing through this room.

I've been at your side for the last twelve days.
You do not stir, even when I squeeze your hand
and tell you about our history.
I sing to you the songs from youth,
as I stroke your auburn hair,
but you do nothing.

I pray that I might kiss your lips
and wake you from your slumber,
but this is not a fairy tale.
Your minutes are numbered
as the doctors come to take the tubes away
and turn the machines off.

I whisper in the darkness secrets
that make my heart race,
afraid to be without you
forty years from now
and longing to give you,
Katie, my only love,
one final kiss.

4 July 2009

WEDDING RING

Despair is searching your soul,
really searching, into every crag or crevice.
Tears streaming down your anguished face
in a quiet Sunday morning bedroom,
with everyone still at church.
No one home to intervene or interrupt
as you come to the startling realization
after thirty two years of contemplation
and rearing three children to adulthood,
and the funding of college degrees with overtime,
and a wedding for the youngest,
and holding his hand in the ambulance
as he had a heart attack,
that you did marry the wrong man after all.

5 April 2009

OUR FIRST MEETING

Hello there.
I've seen your face before,
beautiful as a summer day,
like the day I married the boy next door.
Your eyes, big and blue like my mother's,
a beautiful woman from Sicily,
a true hot blooded Italian,
with a witty retort for her friends,
and fierce as any man,
when she was done wrong.
I bet you're like that too.
I've seen your face before,
I know I have,
your lips small and pink
and delicate as a snowflake,
not thick like mine.
I see that you like to be the center of
attention, the way you light up a room
when you enter,
that's good, you can make that pay
some day, a movie star, or teacher
or leader of your political party,
but there will plenty of time for that,
plenty of time, you'll see.
I can't believe how much you look,
now stop that,
look at you pout,
is that anyway for a lady to act on
such a special day,
pouting.
I can't believe how much you look like
your,
you're doing it again,
your pouting
like your mommy.

8 March 2009

Has husband, needs love, wants boyfriend

Lust

The Pimp of Saint Charles' Brothel

I am the heretic,
the pope in a silk suit,
stenched with perfume from the whores
who worship me,
lost from the fold of society,
imprisoned in my reality
of selling love by the hour
to the lonely businessmen
flush with cash from
closing a big deal,
or a Japanese tourist,
gambling, his
winnings all mine...
in return for
a night of bliss
with two
of the finest
girls
in Las Vegas.

18 November 1987

One Night Stand

We are two strangers
now enveloped
in a tangle of sheets
and arms and legs,
your's silky smooth,
mine covered with hair,
soft and curly.
Two nude bodies
with all our flaws and tattoos
covered in sweat.
Our hearts racing,
matching the other
beat for beat
as
my breath
now synchronized
with yours
makes us a single
body.

You, a beautiful stranger,
I only know
after buying you two
Tanqueray with lime,
in the darkened bar near our University
before you led me onto the dance floor
at half past one this morning.
Your history as foreign to me
as the color of your eyes
or the address on your license,
fake of course.

You arch your back and moan
a sweet obscenity,
though you do not recall my name,
and come morning,
all that shall remain
of our passion tonight
is the memory of another
one night stand.

28 June 2009

Rendezvous

Shadows hide the lies of lovers,
lost in a world of deception
and cast long silhouettes of themselves
on the weathered sidewalk
to be washed away
with the summer downpour
each afternoon at four,
just in time to return to their families,
cleansed
and ready for a cocktail
before supper.

2 June 2009

PERSONAL AD
SWF seeks same

You
soft as a daffodil
standing in a spring rain,
your pedals perfect,
each fold and ripple
moist and delicate,
a photogenic yellow flower,
your pistol spring loaded
sensitive to any guest or invader,
awaiting the warmth of the morning sun
or the western breeze that brings
swarms of pollinators
ready to share.

Me too.

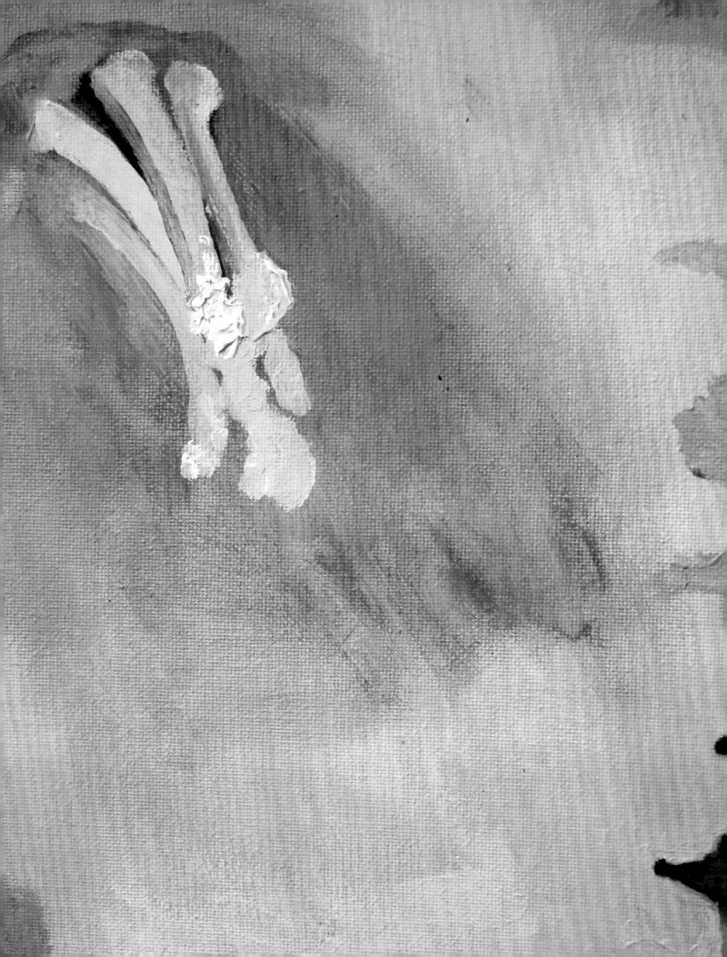

Daddy's Girl

(In remembrance of my father, may he rot in hell.)

My father taught me what I know,
damn bloody bastard.
His promises and pleadings
spent like earnings on whores.
He'd come in darkness.

Hiding his manhood,
slithering maggot on fresh pink meat,
under my blanket of darkness.
He taught me truth.

Bedpost upon my thigh,
icicle spear stinging,
spreading betrayal
through my bones.

Fuck, Fuck, Fuck
Darkness echoing hatred
of purity.
Void.
Loveless pleading.

Three before and two to be
hand raised whores,
ravened haired daughters
of Satan's son.

Fouled life water
spat from little Jew boy
polluting the race,
stained with love.

Pricking, probing ram of battle
Viking's toy destroying the warm
fortress tomb pillaged of memories
yellow nothingness trimmed in moon glow.

Ruby dust on the snow
marking the annals,
another head for the wall,
pristine hide, a throw in the den.

The master must never know.
Mother, rival, whore. I had you soldier
caged in the pocket,
lost from the fight with the rat-tat-tat of life.

Muffled cries, muted laughter,
my prayers and supplication spent.

He'd come in darkness.

9 January 1985

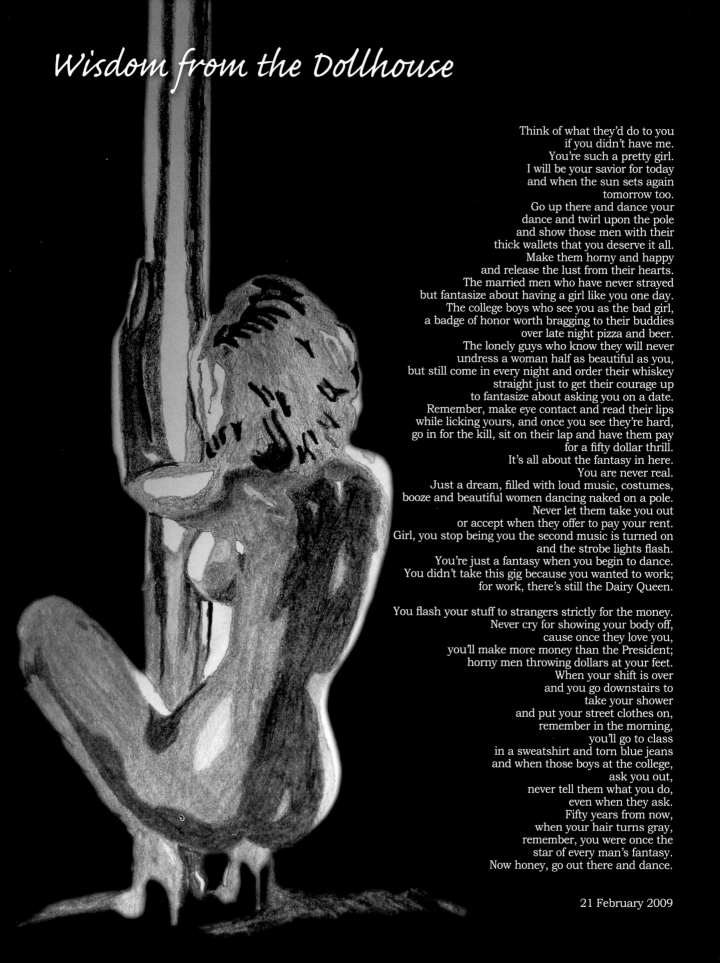

Wisdom from the Dollhouse

Think of what they'd do to you
if you didn't have me.
You're such a pretty girl.
I will be your savior for today
and when the sun sets again
tomorrow too.
Go up there and dance your
dance and twirl upon the pole
and show those men with their
thick wallets that you deserve it all.
Make them horny and happy
and release the lust from their hearts.
The married men who have never strayed
but fantasize about having a girl like you one day.
The college boys who see you as the bad girl,
a badge of honor worth bragging to their buddies
over late night pizza and beer.
The lonely guys who know they will never
undress a woman half as beautiful as you,
but still come in every night and order their whiskey
straight just to get their courage up
to fantasize about asking you on a date.
Remember, make eye contact and read their lips
while licking yours, and once you see they're hard,
go in for the kill, sit on their lap and have them pay
for a fifty dollar thrill.
It's all about the fantasy in here.
You are never real.
Just a dream, filled with loud music, costumes,
booze and beautiful women dancing naked on a pole.
Never let them take you out
or accept when they offer to pay your rent.
Girl, you stop being you the second music is turned on
and the strobe lights flash.
You're just a fantasy when you begin to dance.
You didn't take this gig because you wanted to work;
for work, there's still the Dairy Queen.

You flash your stuff to strangers strictly for the money.
Never cry for showing your body off,
cause once they love you,
you'll make more money than the President;
horny men throwing dollars at your feet.
When your shift is over
and you go downstairs to
take your shower
and put your street clothes on,
remember in the morning,
you'll go to class
in a sweatshirt and torn blue jeans
and when those boys at the college,
ask you out,
never tell them what you do,
even when they ask.
Fifty years from now,
when your hair turns gray,
remember, you were once the
star of every man's fantasy.
Now honey, go out there and dance.

21 February 2009

Man's Desires

How I want to kiss your lips
and undress you slowly by
the flicker of the firelight,
the shadows of lovers upon
a bed.

How I want to embrace you
and feel your hair against my
face, as my lips slowly meet yours,
the down beat of the Bolero
in the air.

How I want to nibble your
breast and feel you quiver
in the excitement of the moment
as you softly moan in the darkness
with each gentle kiss.

How I want to hold you close to me
and feel the warmth of your skin and
the scent of your sweet breath
beneath me as feelings of passion
overtake us.

How I want to feel you writhe in pleasure
as the two of us are joined into one
while you sit on my lap, your naked beauty
exciting me as I fill you with my manhood
and my love.

How I want to envelop you in my arms
and chase your fears away as the
passion of the night stirs our souls until
and at last we fall asleep, a banquet of stars
above us.

1 February 2009

51

MAN'S BEST FRIEND

Not much at first
but there it is.
That which makes us male,
snipped and trimmed
with a mind all its own,
able to find trouble in a convent or brothel.

Impressive in youth,
it wins a scholarship
to university,
where it double majored,
winning accolades
on graduation day.

Once in the real world, it finds friendship
in the oddest places.
Until at last, it is domesticated
and finally comes only on command.

Soon forgotten, it is left to find
contentment on its own,
preferring to remain curled up,
like a hound dog
on a summer porch,
only rewarded on birthdays and anniversaries.
Until, at last, it just lies there
like a mushroom dropped on the sidewalk in August,
unless sprinkled
with the blue fairy dust
advertised
on the television.

11 February 2009

Flight

He recited it with each new affair,
a litany of the women he's been with
since his first kiss.
Said from memory like a prayer
with the pause for contemplation
always at the same place.
The list, shorter than he would want,
but twice as long as most,
filled with the names and faces of the women
whom he loved once or a dozen times.
The beautiful woman with the auburn hair and green eyes
he met touring a castle in Ireland.
And those Greeks and Italians
with the perfect olive complexion,
hair the color of ink,
and large brown eyes
filled with mystery.
He met Gia in the Uffizi, next to The David.
Sofia, he asked directions while drinking Espresso in Capri,
and spent a month on her yacht docked in the harbor.
Dina, the most beautiful woman
he'd ever met, took him on a moonlight walk
on her island with its black volcanic sand
and they made love
under the stars that very night.
The list, filled with plenty of Europeans,
from his days as a pilot for United Airlines,
a jet setter in every sense of the world.
Married thrice – his first, his high school sweetheart,
together until he left the Navy for the sky.
There was the poet from Poland,
with the incredible body that became their common language
until she had the baby and their love grew silent.
Then there was the woman half his age,
a teacher from the Czech Republic,
who bore him three children,
but never one to stay and raise a family,
he strayed and found new love on a business trip to Budapest
where he met an aspiring super model wannabe
searching for an older man to set her dreams free.

There were ladies from Spain and Belgium,
and once a beauty from the Congo,
two from Brazil and two from the Equator
and, of course, the Americans
that he named, unfolding
both hands, extending his fingers,
as he rattled them off like they
were the pride of the '54 Yankees.
Once he finished with his list,
he looked up at the bartender
and with a smile said,
"I guess I'll have another."

Just then a beautiful, big breasted
woman in a pink sweater
sat next to him
and asked with a smile,
"Is this seat taken?"

THE FIRST TIME

How he longed to be passionately embracing her.
His eyes crying out with emotion.
Sex.
He was sixteen and in love.
He had undressed her so many times before
while lying on his bed.
Fantasizing about his lips nibbling
the nipples of her firm breast.
She, gently stroking his hair
while whispering trashing thoughts in his ear,
then her hands slowly sliding down his jeans.
The very thought of his fantasy made him smile.

Tonight was different.
He wasn't fantasizing. Tonight she was really there,
whispering beautiful obscenities, while she nibbled his ear lobes.
It was his dream come true.
The nervous tension hung heavy above them.
How he wanted it to last all night.
How he couldn't wait until he could brag to his basketball buddies
of the glories of this night.
He would be the star of the locker room for next Friday's game.

Then in a sudden burst of unexpected emotion,
his dream, his fantasy come true, came to a crashing halt,
as he jolted upright to see her father
pounding on the glass of his '77 Firebird screaming,

"What the hell are you doing to my daughter?"

1985

54

DOUBT

I placed communion at your lips since you were a teen
and blessed you each Sunday at noon,
on the steps of our church
with your mother beside you,
always in a beautiful dress accented
with jade and gold jewelry,
and of course her diamond, the envy of
every woman in the congregation.

You were just another girl, young and sweet
with budding breast and braces,
chased by boys who invited you to the movies
or a CYO dance on a Friday night
that I chaperoned.

I officiated at your high school graduation
and remember well the words you
spoke as Valedictorian with your perfect GPA
and a scholarship to the College of Villa Maria
to pursue your passion and your voice.

You would stop by the rectory on winter break
to visit with me and tell me of your boyfriends and your studies.
I would share the comfort of the holiday as we talked
in the meeting room outside the secretary's office, and
each year you would give me a gift subscription to the National Geographic.

I remember well when I first noticed you as a woman,
tall and beautiful with a figure that made me pray for understanding
as I spoke with my confessor. That summer that you graduated from Villa Maria,
your family invited me to a bar-b-que and I watched you in the pool,
a drink in my hand and lust in my heart,
trapped in my collar and my vows;
my manhood supposedly extinguished on ordination day
as I lay prostrate before my Bishop.
Never once in twenty years did I ever curse my celibacy,
but I did on that day, my manhood re-ignited, my soul in doubt.

You were so beautiful in that bikini
with your body hard and bronzed,
and I a priest of 46, yet still a man,
capable of lust or love,
regretting that I had only been
with women as a senior in high school,
my midlife crisis
now confronting me.

I regret that I met you for lunch that day at the mall and you asked me
the terrible question that made me rethink my life.

"What is love?"

Flustered and confused I gave you the answer
I had practiced in twenty years of counseling,
but in my state of doubt, I really didn't know.

After lunch you asked me to walk with you near the lake;
you asked me pointed questions and became frustrated at my answers,
but unsure of who I had become.
I ended our conversation
and ran back to my bottle hidden
beneath my breviary
within the solitude of my rectory.

I saw you two weeks later again at that restaurant in the mall,
my answers weren't any better
and it felt strange that someone
I've known forever
could make me rethink the core of my being
with such a simple question,
but that is the power of doubt.

3 February 2009

Prayer brings God's ear to us

Faith

UNCHURCHED

Sunday morning
from nine 'til noon is reserved for us,
the unbeliever, the pagan and the Jew.
We gather at the diner or bagel shop or round the kitchen table
over grits sweet with honey,
and omelets made with scallions and tofu,
or maybe french toast drowning in maple syrup, still warm,
and a thick slab of county ham,
a gift for ourselves from a recent road trip through Virginia
and celebrate this special day,
away from the believers,
in their churches
and all they **say** and do.
The fire and the brimstone,
the praising Hallelujah,
or speaking in tongues with hands raised high,
or the Catholics with their smoke and incense
genuflecting down the aisle,
the born again with the laying on of hands,
bringing the demons out upon command
or the television ministers,
handsome black men all of them,
preaching the holy word for hours,
always starting from a slow boil
pacing themselves at a simmer
before churning their words until they boil over,
sentences flying fast like steam through a locomotive,
causing the congregation to rise in praise and glory
singing Amen's until he reaches the mountain top.
Sunday morning is reserved for us too,
the unchurched,
our favorite day of the week,
quiet and reserved.
We wear t-shirts or a skimpy negligee
as we devour our words in *The New York Times*,
or *Marie Clare* or perhaps the latest Stephen King novel.

We sing alone to the radio while
washing dishes from last night's dinner,
a feast of Thai made from scratch,
for eight of our dearest friends,
or try to keep the sun from waking us
after 10 shots of tequila,
no memory of how we made it to bed,
our own, we hope,
we'll soon find out around noon,
after praying to St. Mattress
a little longer.
Sunday morning gives us three hours
to do what we want,
before the churches let out
and we are once again joined
by our brethren,
dapper, blessed and squeaky clean,
as they join us in line at the Wal-Mart,
or the Outback
or binge bars filling their plates with fried chicken,
and greens and macaroni and cheese
and always a big slice of apple pie before we say
Amen.

8 March 2009

Baptism

Coldness.
Crying.
The church stone solid.
Alone.
A baby lost in the grayness of it all.
Water poured,
a splash of oil,
and a prayer to keep the people happy.

Applause.

Eternal Life.

24 June 1989

Expiation

Each one born to die.
Never to rise,
only to lie.
Cold, rotting, void.
If it were not
for the saving power
of Jesus.

31 January 84

Genesis

Look closely,
beyond the fur,
deeper than the skin,
past the tissue,
into the marrow,
through the microscope,
parsing the strands
of DNA,
unraveling the secrets
they keep,
seeing
the face of God.

13 March 2009

ON THE CROSS

That Friday
she found a sponge
that he soaked
in wine and poison,
an attempt to calm the pain
of their friend.
The afternoon heat
stenched with the foul odor of death
as they raised the sponge on a staff
to moisten the lips
of the condemned man
nailed to that cross above them,
the Romans and spectators mocking him
as a King of the Jews
as he suffocated
with two others
in their own fluids.
The crowd not knowing
that in this time of agony
the weakest among them
would soon change the world.

20 March 2009

SECRET

I pray to know the truth.

You know the truth but still pray.

He prays that the truth may never be known.

Summer 1984

TRANSUBSTANTIATION

The host raised high above his head,
a circle of life,
the body of Christ,
a transformation
of bread
into the body of a savior,
Eucharist.

The pageantry
of candles,
of silk,
of embroidered lace,
of polished metal,
and polished stone,
celebrating this monumental event
faithfully attended by reluctant spectators.
The acolyte ringing bells on cue,
timpani
announcing the entrance of the star,
a sonic boom
warning the congregation of God's appearance
within the sacred symbol
of
total redemption.

A middle age man
sitting in the second pew from the last,
not a Catholic,
came in from the cold,
after walking twenty blocks
trying to clear his head from an early morning fight
with his live-in boyfriend.

The argument,
more than a lover's spat,
not physical or emotional,
but loud and awkward
in their paper-walled apartment
about the money spent on birthday presents
for his sister.
The boyfriend angry at such excess,
when they had been twice late on the apartment rent.

The visitor in the pew
wanting
simply to show his love
for his sister

in a way she'd always remember
on her fiftieth.
A gift of an heirloom map of Paradise
for her collection.
Its price,
more than he could easily afford,
a sacrifice
he wanted to make,
a tribute to the sister who raised him
from the day
their mother died.

Take this all of you and eat it, this is my body.

The echo of the bells
vibrating
throughout the sanctuary.
The priest saying his sacred prayers
as he
slowly
places
the circle of life
on the gold patent sitting on the altar.

The visitor allowing the words from the altar to fade
as he concentrated on the conversation in his head,
confused
as why the boyfriend,
an agonistic,
was still so angry
at such a precious gift given to the person
that was so important to him.

The congregation rising,
he makes his escape
out to the cold,
as the organist begins
to play
the beautiful music
he remembered hearing
as a kid
living near the Cathedral of Saint Peter
in Scranton.

24 February 2009

PEBBLES

The story of a
life isn't a postcard
to be saved in a box
with all the dusty memories
that a life well lived accumulates.

Nor is it a sculpture of polished stone
honed to a shimmer in abstract form
placed on a pedestal in a garden of water lilies,
their white flowers floating on the surface of still black water
for the world to appreciate in quiet reverence and contemplation.

No, life is so much more than pretty.
A long life is beautiful in its complexity,
but only from a distance.
While living it, it is little more than
a billion stones, and shards of glass, hard and rough and dangerous,
mixed with fragments of copper and gold
and here and there a diamond or emerald
or amethyst protruding from its jagged geode, painful to touch.
Life, when viewed at death, reveals itself to be a mosaic of the pebbles,
some polished soft by the waves of time,
others a hard as a grain of sand or fragile as a snowflake,
that made up our day to day.

The mosaic, laid down one pebble at a time,
is filled with the color and texture,
the pains and sorrows, and whatever joys the artist was able to capture
until the picture of life is revealed only at their departing.
More than a random pattern of waves and undulations,
laid out before the viewer, but a picture as beautiful
as a thousand acres of the finest Dutch tulips
or as useless television static after the signal goes out.
Each person we encounter on our journey
is a pebble in our mosaic,
some polished smooth, others rough cut,
the artist never knowing the most important stone
until
the last one is laid
at final breath.

17 March 2009

Steeples on Christmas

They rise into the morning sky,
their crosses glimmering in the early light,
their buildings still bathed in blackness,
when the first bells begin to chime
this cold December morn.
The world awakes to celebrate the birth of the savior
in churches for their own,
the Baptist, the Methodist,
the Anglican and the Lutheran build
mighty churches all of them,
but the Catholic.
Oh, the Catholic.
They build them by the acre,
cathedrals made of stone,
with spires rising to the sky,
trying to reach right to heaven,
protecting their members when they die
by topping them with crosses
so each passerby will know the reason
this city has so many churches,
as they walk on Christmas morning
to celebrate with family
the birth of their baby savior,
his star glimmering in the early light
to a world bathed in darkness
in a land so far away.
They say he
came to save us,
but
that was a long, long time ago.

9 February 2009

Paralyzed in 1992, Christopher has taught himself to paint by holding paintbrush in his mouth.

Even bullies cry when momma dies

Death

IN PRAISE OF DEATH

As fast as the wind that escorts the summer storms,
it shall come.

The same way it came for Moses, Jesus and Gandhi,
it shall grow near.

The same way it grew near for Alexander, Nero and Hitler,
it shall fall upon us.

Forts of iron and treasures of gold.
All are powerless against its might.
Man has run from its power
and hid from its doom.
Yet, he was still powerless.

With the suddenness of a match upon kindling, it strikes.
With the deliverance of a gem cutter at the stone, it lingers.

It takes its child by the hand,
leading it forth transing two worlds from darkness to doom,
doom to glory.

Foolish man.
Run not, hide not.
Life must die as death must live.

1980

MADD

The doctor enters the room solemnly,
his eyes conveying the worst fear,
now confirmed,
that every parent hides beneath their soul,
praying that it always remains sequestered for eternity.
Until the night in leaks out
after a summer bonfire down by the lake,
fueled by a couple of cases of Carona and
two bottles of Jack Daniels whiskey,
and the long ride home on that country road
black as ink for the first twenty miles.

4 June 2009

She Looks So Peaceful

The casket was there
as were the candles and tears
and the chubby ladies in their
black clothes,
sophisticated, but not evening wear.
A testament that the old lady in the box traveled
among the right social circles,
or rather
her children did.

Truth told, few gathered around her casket had ever
met the well quaffed women with the glasses perched
at the bridge of her long thin nose.
A gold broach pinned
over her left breast.

They knew the stories about her, told by her children to fellow
co-workers, and bridge partners, dates and club members.
They knew she was a Democrat, a liberal, a non-smoker.
She raised orchids and baked cherry pies with lace crust so
light and fluffy, she'd won the praises of all her friends and relatives
but never a blue ribbon; she didn't believe in contests.

She dressed well and lived within her means, no summer house
on the lake, or at the shore. She liked to ski,
but wasn't very good at driving in snow.
She bought union made and drove a Chevrolet,
even after her children were driving Lexus's.
She didn't drink anything more than white wine on evenings out
and a glass of sherry or merlot with dinner in the kitchen.

Two hundred faces gathered in the great old funeral home in the center of town,
but only Uncle Leo and her husband and the five children she raised
into their fifties could say they knew her,
but then only as sister, wife and mother.

There were grandchildren, twelve of them, who knew her as a grandmother, who
sent five dollar bills in birthday cards and attended ballet recitals
and band concerts, graduations and Sunday dinners.

Long gone were loves and lovers from her youth.

Absent was the mustached man with the double breasted suit
and thick black hair combed back to emphasize dark green eyes
that she stared into deeply, lovingly, on lazy Sunday mornings
as a sophomore at Vassar after they made love in his tiny apartment.

Long ago buried was the married philosopher whom she tryst with for ten years
while in her thirties. How she'd loved discussing ethics and religion
over pots of strong tea, piping hot, spiked with bourbon.
How she had longed for his embrace nearly every day of the last fifty-four years,
never once uttering a whisper about him.

Missing too was the kindly old Polish woman who lived in the apartment beneath her
and drove her to Westchester on a beautiful October morning in 1950
to rid the problem left behind by a cowardly boyfriend.

Just a faded memory captured in a photo,
framed next to her was the stern father
in the thick wool suit with a gold pocket watch
and small round spectacles
that focused on his small round head.
Next to him, a young thin woman in long white gloves
and a crisp gray dress holding an infant;
the woman herself now deceased.

Gone as well were her sisters,
Elizabeth, Heidi, Florence and Rose Mary.
Buried with them were lies and laugher,
jealousies and sorrows found within a sister's love.

She held a doctorate,
but absent this day were her students
who praised her teaching
during forty years of lectures
and labs and chemistry experiments
at colleges and universities with ivied walls
and prestigious names
scattered throughout New England.

Left to shed the tears were her sons,
Felix and Malcolm,
standing and greeting those at the front of the reception line
with their wives and children.
Closest to the dark oak box
with the double quilted upholstery
and the burnished brass handles
were her daughters
and her husband,
who never thought he'd outlive her.
Seated in his wheel chair,
a white handkerchief
supported by a gnarled aged hand,
his eyes closed and moist from tears
and his voice
little more than a hollow whisper.

"She looks so peaceful."

Each mourner would say out of respect.
Simple words left behind to honor a life
that they didn't really know
as they walked past
the casket of the gray haired women
in the purple dress
sleeping
with glasses on.

16 January 2009

THE LAST ACRE

Chosen as the best place to bury their generations,
selected because it's high and always dry,
and offered a view of the creek where the blue jays
danced in the summertime.

Down from the house and barns
and away from the live stock pens with the
foul odor that grows thick with lack of
wind common 'round here in the hot days of August.

Near the hedge row of trees, oak and ash,
reflecting on the great silver pond
filled with tadpoles each April
turned to bullfrogs by July.

Guarded by a field stone fence three feet high
and two feet wide, the final repository for the granite
stones found by every generation who plowed with
oxen, mule, draft horse and for the last sixty years, Deere.

Entered through a rod iron gate more than a hundred years old,
so heavy it gives a great creak each time it swings open
to let in the mourners burying the aged dead or
laughing children trying to hide behind a weathered stone.

Every generation to toil on this rich soil has taken comfort in
knowing that when their final days are done,
they will be returned to the land that made them what they were
a well respected member of this community and a steward of their land.

And as I walk with my grandson holding my calloused hand, my gray hair
blowing in the autumn breeze, I know that when my winter comes, I will join
them all, seven generations of farmers, remembered by future generations,
guarded by a granite wall, at rest, at last, their harvest in,
once they reached the last acre.

14 February 2009

CONDEMNED

The stone drops quick
bringing the condemned with it
as together they splash and disappear
beneath the cold, gray water,
a glaze of ice floating at the surface.
The judge issued his verdict
and the townspeople carried it out,
under a cold November sunrise,
for the murder of a five year old girl,
who vanished the day before
and was found near a stream
by the minister's wife and three others on the search,
the condemned man cradling her bloodied body
and crying inconsolably.

The man, a stranger, with no business here,
and a thick accent from a country still under a czar's rule,
was pronounced guilty by evening,
no lawyer to proclaim his innocence,
or reason to believe he came upon the child
dead in the stream as he asserted tearfully,
only anger filtering the air of the makeshift courtroom,
the town's meeting hall, a fire burning in the hearth,
warming the room, already hot with hatred,
as the elder, a man with thick white hair that gave wisdom to his words,
listened, his lips silent, as he heard the story told
and issued his sentence,
calming the crowd with his quotation of Exodus 21:23-27
and the rendering of an eye for an eye.

28 June 2009

MONTANA MOURNING

My Sunday suit returned to
a Thursday morning closet.

Darkness gives birth to a pink and purple sky
as I stare through the kitchen sink window,
a heavy mug of coffee steaming
in my cowboy hands.
Mist rising from the river,
near where the fence post was forced down.

Deep ruts now scar my land.

Spring will be here soon.
The frozen river will run strong
with trout and salmon,
and fathers will teach their boys
to cast
in these cold waters,
lessons learned in patience
and disappointment.

The icy land will yield to spring
as purple flowers dance
along the river's edge filling the sorrow in.
Soon forgotten,
a father's frantic cry for help;
his boy lost through the ice.

Those rocks out there – where the tears froze
to my face – will soon be covered
from the spring thaw
and once again brown bears
will perch upon them
with pink bellied fish shimmering
from their mouths.

And I will always hear the screams
lost in the waves rushing down the river
from the mountain top
as I look out on Montana in morning.

8 October 2008

ON DEATH AND OTHER MATTERS OF LIFE

The frozen pillow sits,
lost on the green desert whispering,
"We are lovers no longer."
Sleeping in silence like that fish on the mantle piece,
at last you're useless.
Your breakfast cereal floats in the sink, a monument to your being.
Only the hanger hangs,
longing for the blue silk suit and that gaudy polyester tie;
you know the one,
with the khaki grapefruit
and the Harvard hued letters peddling Florida.
The one your mother brought home when you were twelve.
I've contained my sorrow in the crushed Salems
scattered across our water bed.
The morning has come... perhaps today I shall philosophize
about life while swallowing my stale yellow reality
with my mourning's Mary.
The county coroner found a photo of your cow breasted bitch sitting on the hood of your car,
a dozen roses across her skirt.
She's more of a spider than a broad.
I thought you could do better than that.
Hell, I did.

Well, I'm freed of this chocolate covered nightmare.
Remember when the vinyl of your father's prized Nash,
the cold crisp snap of skin fighting to be stained,
killed the star light feeling.
Thus I feel again.

I want to go home.

16 January 1985

Marble on the Hill

Think of what I will become
when they are finished with the incense and holy water.
After the flowers and flag have been removed
and the mourner's tears dried.

Think of what I will become after my widow spends
sleepless nights crying my name
and my children have returned to their families
in distant cities reached only every once in a while
by a birthday card or e-mail,
never a phone call, not since their children were born
and time at last evaporated from their lives.

Think of the stories that will be remembered by my friends, but never shared.
What will come of the lives that once I touched each day,
the doorman, the waitress and the postman
whose name I never learned - twenty years of smiles stuffed between
bills and magazines?

What will become of my reputation as a doctor, teacher, father, husband?
Will the golf pro remember my name as he recounts how I made a hole-in-one on my birthday,
or the father when he tells his son how I saved his life after that horrible accident that claimed
his mother and his wife?
Who will remember my lovers, conquests and one night stands from my youth,
affairs of the heart from my graying years?
The day I met my second wife, at the funeral of my first.

In the end, is the noble work of scholar and physician,
beggar and burglar weighed from the same scale? Is all that remains of all of us
nothing more than dust, lost in context from the life once lived?
Is the truth, never spoken in temple, mosque or cathedral,
nothing more than we will all be lost to the abyss of time?

Think of what I will become
when they are finished with the incense and holy water,
after the flowers and flag have been removed
and the tears dried.

Will I become nothing more than marble on the hill?
Fighting for attention with all the others,
seventy years of life condensed to polished stone
lost among so many.
Millionaires and patriots forced to
build so grand in order to demonstrate
they even existed.

18 November 2008

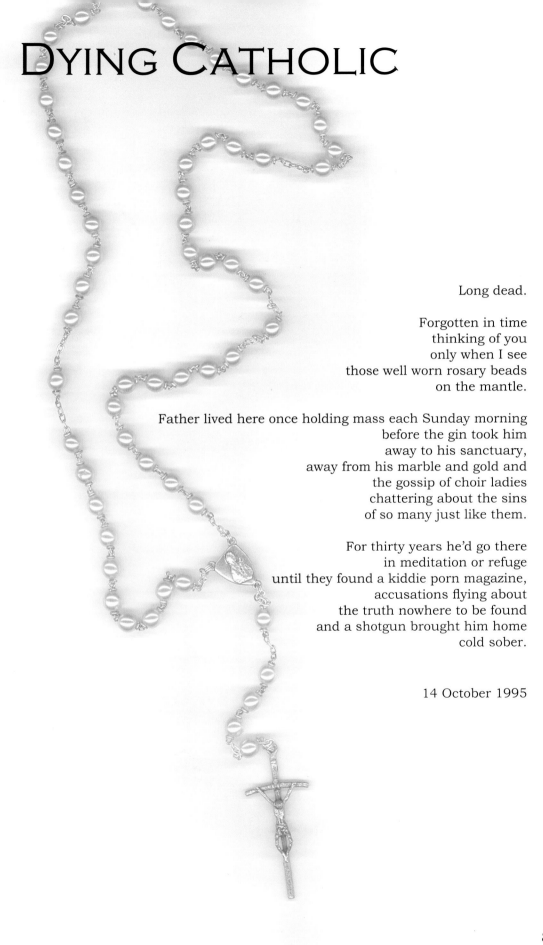

Dying Catholic

Long dead.

Forgotten in time
thinking of you
only when I see
those well worn rosary beads
on the mantle.

Father lived here once holding mass each Sunday morning
before the gin took him
away to his sanctuary,
away from his marble and gold and
the gossip of choir ladies
chattering about the sins
of so many just like them.

For thirty years he'd go there
in meditation or refuge
until they found a kiddie porn magazine,
accusations flying about
the truth nowhere to be found
and a shotgun brought him home
cold sober.

14 October 1995

KILLING THE PATIENT

He was his own worst patient,
the chief of the thoracic surgery at
a prestigious mid-western hospital
with an ego to match the board room
he called his private office, photos and
trophies adoring the walls celebrating
his very being.

A larger than life beast of a man
with long slender fingers capable
of playing Gershwin to entertain his friends,
keeping him the center of attention
when not removing an inoperable
tumor from some famous patient
who flew in from Berlin.

A pain in his hip that his pills didn't cure
was why he ordered the x-ray which showed
blackness throughout his bones and took
his breath away.

For forty years, he diagnosed and issued
the horrible news to others with the strength
of a savior; their personal deity who promised
to save them from the terrible fate that lesser
hands from God could not. And now he realized
that as patient, he was little more than a victim
counting the clicks of the second hand
waiting for his watch to stop.

He studied the scans and x-rays
and knew the terrible truth.
With luck he would have six months
of life before he'd be little more than a corpse
waiting for agonizing pain and suffering to end.

He would have none of this;
death by agony was not in his plan.
God could have him, but not like this.
He would leave this life as a dignified man,
with Verdi playing in the background
in his comfortable bed with his wife and his friends
and his mistress of twenty years beside him.

He ordered the pills
he would need to control his plan.
Morphine tablets
he could administer by hand.
He stockpiled them in a jar
on the small table beside the bed
which he took from the hospital,
two each week,
a token to count his remaining days
of productivity and freedom.

When at last that day had come,
and his frame was oversized for
skin that remained draped over it,
the shape of his bones poking through
and the hair dye long gone showed
thin and gray, and his face gaunt and
hollow and his clear blue eyes
once bright now dark with pain
that echoed throughout his being.

He knew that at last that day had come.
He would cheat death of agony but
only by a week or two,
for his agony had been growing
like that of a rising tide
approaching a boy trapped in the sand,
certain to drown, but when.

With all of his family and friends
in the living room beneath him,
he prepared the death potion,
three burnt orange pills at a time
chased by a mouthful of Klipdrift brandy.
He repeated this ritual a dozen times, ensuring
that he ingested double the dose required to kill him.
A man always in charge, he didn't want to recede
into a coma, his plan halfway done.

His wife knew of his plan
and once she finished holding
his hand and kissing his brow,
summoned for the guests
below to enter.

There were ten in all,
his closest friends,
who gathered around
the antique poster bed.
Absent was his only daughter
whom he disowned thirty years before
for marrying an uneducated black boy
and boring him black babies
that shamed their family name.

He spoke briefly and thanked them all
for their love and friendship
then took a giant sigh.
He closed his eyes and lost his smile.

His breath slowed
then the heaving of his chest slowed
and the stirring within the room grew silent,
except
for the final notes
of Verdi's Requiem Mass.

Within a few minutes the room slowly emptied,
except for
his wife
and
his mistress,
who remained there silent
holding the man they both loved.

4 February 2009

BURIAL IN A COUNTRY CEMETERY

Five horses stand tied to the hitching post,
their carriages empty and still, while
a mist falls from the October sky, gray
as a beautiful mare.
Outside the elegant stonewall erected
to keep death contained
so that we might have a place to visit
it, before it chooses to repay the kindness
and visit us.
We mark the spot we bury our dead
with polished stone, mere markers for the benefit
of the deceased, so they might
remember who they were when they
rise with the second coming.
Today, the grave is deep, the earth showing
veins of clay, orange and purple worked tightly between
rocks and roots and the marks of the gravedigger's shovel
The wail of three orphans, heartfelt dirges
bring somberness to this hallowed earth, while the parson
recites the Psalms as the caskets are lowered into the hole
and the ground is quickly returned to ground.

24 August 2009

In war, silenced voices speak loudest

War

ARLINGTON NATIONAL CEMETARY

Stone soldiers
tattooed with bravery,
sentries of freedom
sleeping silently
in their dress uniforms
after devil's work.

Their spot of grass
crew cut according to
regulation 1749.B.

Only tears and memories
left on white monuments
marshaled into tight
rows
of platoons,
and regiments,
and divisions,
and conflicts,
and decades,
and centuries.

Here
three hundred thousand lives
honored in waves
of white
celebrating
the Freedom of a Nation
with the death of so much promise
by the flags placed in front of every
stone on Veteran's Day
as the sounds of taps echoes
in the air this beautiful
autumn morning.

21 October 1995

A Simple Tribute

They fought the fight to free that land
from being reaped by the sickle
or pounded by the hammer.
Over a flag of red, they died.

For sixteen years, we sent our sons over
to do the right thing.
For sixteen years, they sent our sons back
in plastic bags or small wooden caskets.

They died not in war, but in a police action,
yet they wore the uniform of soldiers

Those who died where buried with their brothers
in rows of white simple markers as their only tribute.

Eight years have faded since those days of pain.
Those baby faced boys have evolved into men
who cry at the remembrance of that crazy
war where in the end no one emerged a winner.

They will stare into a polished granite wall marking
the lives of the numbered dead, placing their fingers
on the etched black stone to become whole again
someday, someday.

1982

VJ DAY

Landmines, hand grenades, and bullets
by the case quickly bulldozed into a pit
dug for the occasion
and coated with napalm
spread thick as apple butter
ignited at five minutes past midnight
to celebrate the signing
of the Documents of Surrender
on the Battleship Missouri.
The realization by all of us,
weary and exhausted
from years of fighting
in the jungles and pacific atolls
that perhaps now we are not going to die
as young men after all.

13 February 2009

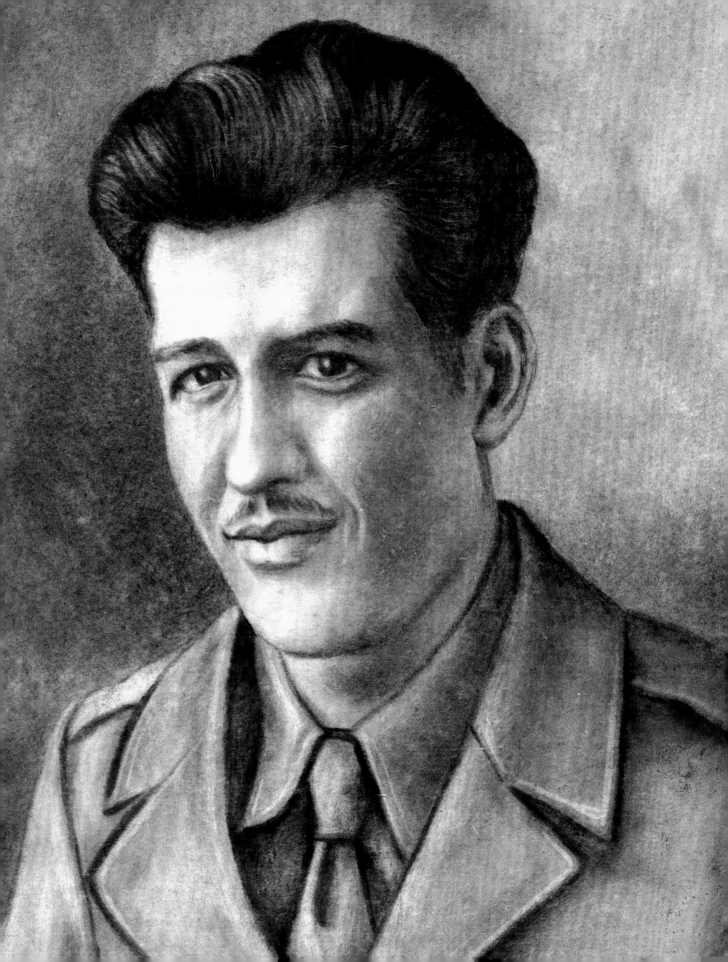

Bronze Star

They don't teach men to be heroes
or lovers or saints. They train them
simply to be killers, cold, matter-of-fact killers,
molded from depression-era boys ready to
make a difference with their young lives.

They don't teach them to die for their county;
they show them how to use a Browning automatic rifle
to persuade the enemy to die for his.

They never teach men to stare into the hazel eyes
of their best friend and cradle him
as the blood spurts out of his temple onto
your face, rough as shale,
dripping with blood and brain
and salty sweat as you both gasp for breath
in the inferno hell of this Pacific atoll,
the adrenaline pumping as you watch him die,
cut down by the sniper's bullet
meant for you and not cry?

They don't teach men to be heroes
while fighting on the coral rock called Peleliu,
its blood drenched earth hard and painful,
as those around you die one by one
under a moonlit sky,
killed by the unseen enemy,
living like ants in a colony of caves
that even overwhelming forces can not exterminate.

They don't teach men to protect their friends
stranded by weeks of unending combat,
their ammunition spent, forced to forage for bullets
and finding nothing but twelve cases of hand grenades
which lobbed into the darkness throughout the night
protect their comrades
wounded or dying until they can be rescued in daylight.

They don't teach men to find the strength
to remain brave in the midst of such unwinnable odds
as the stench of death from ten thousand dead
hangs heavy in the air of that rock
less than six miles square.

They don't teach men to be heroes, or lovers
or saints. He was simply born one.

9 September 2009

Dedicated to Anthony Joseph Ferrandi, Private with the 81st Infantry Division, 321st Regiment Combat Team, who was awarded the Bronze Star for extraordinary valor in the Battle of Peleliu

Colonel Sherman

Sleep well Colonel Sherman.
The old gray photo is still there perched upon the mantelpiece,
a blanket of dust to keep it warm.
The pride of his mother's side uniform
He made it through THE POINT on horseback
and was shipped to San Juan to prevent those spics from unhappiness.
He fell in love with a brown skinned one
and was sent to Wisconsin to gather his wits about him.
He was in the Army now.
Not a boy, a lover, a man.
Just a soldier with saddle sores
and a friend between his legs.
No need for a woman yet
to nurture and serve
and save him from himself
on a distant battlefield.

He was a soldier's soldier in shiny black boots with thick black soles
and bright brass buttons across his uniform that matched his hair.

WESTPOINT

An old man with a passion for life that had served him well
in so many battles mapped across his chest,
a favorite storyteller to the cadets.
He'd smile and laugh as he undid his big buttons to reveal his favorite scars,
each one with a different tale,
a bloody ending
and then his laughter would evaporate
while he shed a single tear
for a long lost friend.

Then he'd begin again,
Moving to the next one showing his life stitched and tattooed
and scarred across his large blonde belly.
He was regular army all the way.

No time for much of anything except
molding young, blonde hair, farm boys into
high stepping monuments to himself.
One day The Point will raise a stone to him,
A hero from the Great War who fell at last
A solder to the last
finally retreating to eternity.

20 August 1988

J. Barnum 09

Productivity without happiness is worthless prosperity.

Work

APPALACHIAN AUTUMN

The leaves are all gone now
and so are the visitors and lovers,
blankets spread under canopies of
birch and maple, elm and oak,
their fiery leaves dappled on
a warm, sunny Saturday
while children danced in the wood
gathering perfect specimens
colored firethorn and gold
for grandmothers to press between a
thick volume of Elizabethian love poems,
its tattered leather hard as old skin.

Since the last full moon, the white tail bucks are in rutting now,
racing through these woods in search of a mate or two.
Their carcasses spread along of the side of the interstate
like mile markers,
soon to be heaved into dump trucks
by young black men in blue jumpsuits
on work release.

The days are growing colder
and I find myself grabbing that warm gray sweater
after putting on my father's old flannel shirts each morning,
a constant reminder that we do evolve into our fathers,
even academics, who've lost their footing after cancer
and then a divorce and two children, bitter that I've survived both.

All alone I sit by a cast iron stove
feeding it wood hourly
and think and write for my publisher
about love and poetry and moonbeams
until I am so tired
that I must masturbate myself to sleep
after praising the Appalachian autumn
for the editors of *The Washington Post*
to have by deadline.

25 October 2008

Following the Marlboro Man

Tobacco hangs from the rafters
of the huge weathered barns,
their siding planks turning silver
in the autumn sun
until the leaves, dried,
now the color of brown suede
are ready to be packed onto farm trucks driven
by the sons' of farmers,
in their dungarees
and Grateful Dead t-shirts
and blue Converse high tops,
their driver's licenses
as new as a kiss.
Thursday afternoon,
this scene repeated throughout the tobacco country
of Charles, Prince George's and
Anne Arundel Counties,
as sons follow convoys
lead by their fathers in their bib overalls
down Maryland Route 301
to the yearly tobacco auction
held in Upper Marlboro.

14 February 2009

Giving a Bath to the Insane

Her hands tremble slowly,
as they have for the last fifty two years
until their movement,
involuntary,
has become part of her being,
like the face that never smiles
or the eyes that stared only forward
while her lips, cracked and small,
and always silent
lock her dreams away.
She sits most days on the wooden chair with the high back,
built in the Shaker style and stares through the finger printed glass
overlooking the commissary, searching for the face of God.

On Wednesdays, she wanders the grounds
of the hospital with its once manicured lawns,
now in bloom with dandelions,
their whispering puffs of seed blossoms
blowing in the breeze,
as Lady Charlotte, the seventy year old
woman, thinking herself to be a girl of eight
chases after them.

In the evening, an orderly, most likely Charles,
a beautiful Jamaican with dreads tied in a pony tale,
brings her to me.
I slowly undress her, attempting to preserve her
dignity while revealing her nudity
in the shower room of thick gray marble,
its echoing always unsettling to the patients.

Her bones too frail for a shower,
I bath her each evening in
the bathtub twenty years older than she,
filled with tepid water,
the proper temperature important,
never too hot or too cold
always tepid,
so not to awaken memories too painful for tears.
I wash her aged body with soap and a cloth,
but she never moves or acknowledges that I have invaded
her privacy, even when I wash her breast,
small as spoonful, or scrub her behind, before coating it in
ointment and baby powder. Each night I pull the nightgown,
always cotton, its thickness changing with the seasons,
over her wrinkled face still unmoved by
my compassion for her after thirty years of kissing her forehead
after tucking her in her bed.

22 April 2009

Six words
that changed the lives of an entire town of a quarter million,
the pain as thick as ink left on the knives used to coat the rollers,
the printing press still warm,
unaware of the tragedy that occurred this day.
The printing plates savaged from the massive press
with the image of the pages burned on each plate,
a moribund souvenir to be displayed in family restaurants and club basements for decades.
Below the fold,
a cover story about the dismal economy
and the wars and the indictment of a county councilmen.
Page two featured an exposé about a bank failure down in Springfield
and opposite it, a full page from Macy's announced the closing of their store at the mall,
with its 50% off sale, a sign of the turbulent times.
The rest of the A section, just wire copy.
The metro and the sports section too thin to wrap much fish,
just a dozen ads and ten articles, mostly fluff or stories from The Associated Press
and a couple of ball scores, only the obituaries and the legal notices
deep with bankruptcies and foreclosures filling the pages.
Wordsmiths, a baker's dozen,
most freshly minted from J school,
follow the middle aged mother,
who has covered the local art scene since a stringer in high school,
and two gray haired men,
veterans both of Vietnam and too many cigarettes,
one the managing editor,
who had walked every inch of the city
in thirty two years of covering crime and corruption
and the evolution of this town from acres of plum trees
to sprawling subdivisions,
their residents too busy to read the words published each morning for a quarter,
and the sports reporter who has covered two generations of high school teams,
knighting princes with his prose,
covering yearly state championships
from archery to wrestling
and once an Olympic high diver
who brought the town to their feet
after she won the silver,
her picture splashed across the Sunday edition,
walk from their red brick office
in a light rain carrying cardboard boxes,
their faces filled with emotion and tears
summed up with the final morning headline,
FRIENDS, WORDS CAN'T SAVE US NOW.

20 March 2009

LANDMAN

It's never with pride they decide to plant neat rows of houses,
although I do my best to ease the pain.
My grandfather's great grandfather came from Germany
and cleared this land more than seven generations ago,
I'm always told.
The place is little more than a humble farm
with a small Sears mail order house perched
on deep rich soil that grew tomatoes, beans, and pumpkins,
staples for America sold at their farm stand
or from the bed of a faded green pick-up truck parked along the paved road.

On the last acre, near the birch tree,
they're all buried on the same ground where they toiled,
Jacob and Eli, Jonah and Greta, Elizabeth and the baby she lost in childbirth,
two hundred years of kin in all.
From dust to dust, those words were lived through drought
and scorching sun,
and when they prayed for rain,
and it finally came,
it washed the soil away
and left marshes of mud that anchored their John Deere tractor to the earth.

There were the bumper crops,
once a decade or so,
when the melons grew so large that it took two boys to lift them to the truck,
but no other business could thrive with just three good years outta ten.
Those boys are grown now, off the farm,
a banker in Boston, a teacher to the blind.
The daughters too have married and moved away to Colorado, Houston and Taipei.

And so that call is made to me
to sell the farm for their family.
I must tell the builders it's time to plant neat rows of plastic covered boxes
in the tomato field where young families will tend to little gardens
and nurture their children on the cul-du-sac.

And when the time comes for the farmer down the way to call me too,
he will be protested by new neighbors, driving their SUV's and
wearing their Birkenstocks and living in their plastic coated boxes
filled with organic fabrics and landscaped lawns
topped with little signs proclaiming,
it's time to save the farmers from themselves
and stop this crazy sprawl.

But soon there will be new families wanting to live their American dream
with tomatoes and beans and pumpkins in their backyard
and a flag of stars and stripes waving proudly in the breeze
next to their SUV's.

And though I hate to see another family farm fall,
I take comfort in doing my job well,
like the undertaker and the butcher.
All my farmers know that one day too,
they will make that call and
I will represent them when they sell, and
yes, together we will count the money,
but it's never with pride
they decide to plant neat rows of houses,
although I do my best to ease their pain,
just like the first drops of a summer rain.

7 November 2008

101

LOUDER THAN WORDS

The pigtailed teen wrote on her resume that she knew sign language,
an elective she took in high school; a skill she mastered
signing pop songs with the radio.

Summoned to a doctor's office from her basement department,
where the doctors printed their money, sending out bills for
PAP smears and colored pills, colon exams and blood transfusions.

The young clerk walked across the campus of the big city hospital
into an exam room where a doctor, bald and fat, stood in a
fine wool suit, with a starched white shirt with purple cuff links
that matched his new silk tie, framed by an open lab coat.

"You speak sign language?" he said,
like it was Turkish, Russian or German.

"I sign."

On a cold silver table,
sat a middle aged woman,
nude, with sagging breast,
wrapped in a blue paper robe.

"This is Mrs. Zanivich.
She has cancer,"
the doctor said, forgetting he was human.

Through the girl, the doctor
spoke of pancreatic abnormalities,
grim prognoses, little time for experimental treatments
and life ending consequences.

The woman sat in silence, the word
CANCER racing from her fingertips,
tears streaming past her dark red lips.

The girl too cried,
silence
and
flashing fingers their common bond.

"Is he saying I'm going to die?"

The girl's hands remained frozen,
but her tear filled eyes did not lie.

"Is he saying I'm going to die?"

It won't be long, her fingers flashed
stage four, no time for much, a little suffering,
a month or two, but medication should keep the pain at bay,
her choice, home or in the hospital, it's all the same.

The girl and the woman spoke with their eyes
as their fingers fell silent.
The doctor too was silent,
but only because he had nothing more to say.

Tears streamed from two women
bonded by pain
as the sound of the fluorescent light
and the smell of disinfectant
polluted the room
and the doctor left
to take a new patient.

22 January 2009

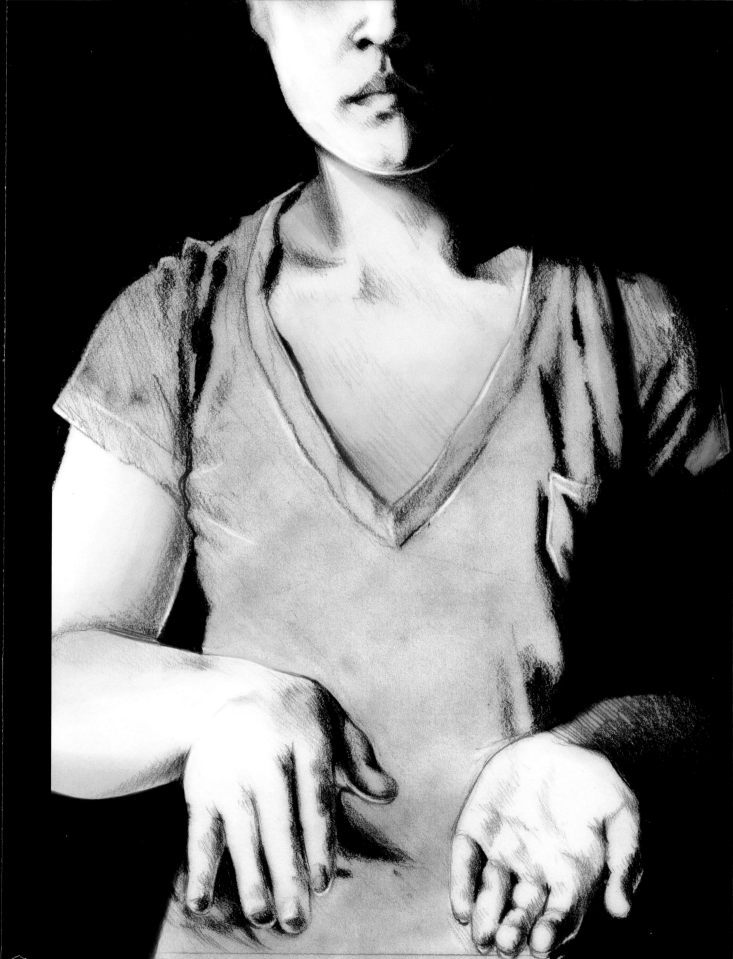

IN THE FAMILY CAR

I am the nameless, faceless driver
in my mourning clothes each day.
My clients never want to know me
when I take them to that dreadful
place and back, tearing
families missing one of their own.
The ritual of honoring a life lived
full cycle to be returned
from whence it came. I am the driver
of the family car, polished black
and silver with the name of my employer,
Sullivan's Funeral Home,
hand lettered on the back.
I know where the bodies are buried for I hear
the gossip and the tales
between wails of a young mother's
sorrow and despair and an aged grieving
woman, now a widow, alone in her world
for the first time in sixty years. I see the
parents holding their babies tightly as we
drive by the scene of the accident
where their grandfather died.
In the privacy of the family car,
they tell the stories of why a daughter has
been left from the will, or who his father really was,
private matters released in grief or
a slip of the lip to ease the pain.
In hushed tones they air the family secrets
or complain about the
God damn nursing home that
sucked grandfather dry and with it their inheritance.
I hear it each way with my eyes facing forward
and my head hung low. They never tell me, but
I know about the sinners and saviors of our
town, just west of Boston.
Five days each week,
I drive the Catholic, the Baptist and the Jew
to their loved one's final rest. Mine is the family car
and they never ask my name.

8 February 2009

TWEEDS

Businessmen travel in packs,
swaggering, but not like lions;
laughing, but not like coyotes,
not even in swarms or gaggles or schools.
The white breasted pinstripe makes its own crowd
hiding beneath the soften tweeds of success.
Lying to each other about conquest,
framed with a pocket square.
Nesting in the comforts of tickertape,
tax forms and telephones,
until the gold watch is awarded
in their gray hair years.

S.J. Ferrandi
Written with
Kate Wing
Summer
1989

WATER WITCH VOLUNTEER FIRE COMPANY

I cried that Christmas twenty years ago.

The smell of smoke still thick in my lungs,
my tongue black with soot and my ears
ringing with the cries of a daughter
screaming for her mommy,
lost in a corner of her bedroom,
the air too thick to breath,
paralyzed by fear and fire
and then,
a stranger walking through it all
offering to save her as she cowered in that corner,
her teddy bear and her Barbie protected in her arms.
My face mask feeding me air that I now shared with her,
as I lifted her from the floor
and placed her over my shoulder,
fire all around us
until we reached the kitchen door,
and saw the flashing strobe lights from the apparatus,
punching through the darkness of the clear winter sky,
the temperature twenty degrees below freezing,
ice covering the ruins of that farmhouse
as I walked past the bodies of my brother and his wife
laid out near his pick up truck.
Me, holding his only daughter,
trying to comfort the little girl I held at her baptism,
Fr. Sullivan blessing her with chrism and holy water,
as I vowed to protect her from the darkness and evil of this world,
but now,
all I can do is kiss her forehead and tell her I love her
on that horrible Christmas morning.

15 June 2009

Washington, D.C. 1972

Snowflakes dance in the whirlwind beneath the street light
plastered with an upside down Nixon bumper sticker along its shaft.
Two hookers, cousins in real life,
in too tight black leather mini skirts
and fishnet stockings ripped along the seams,
wearing matching white cotton tops,
so shear they show the weave of their bras,
stand beneath the flickering lamp,
their makeup pancaked thick as cold cream
over their haggard black faces,
perhaps trying to hide the pain
earned earlier that day at the hand of their pimp,
now sitting in his bright orange Cadillac
hidden in a darkened alley across from them,
for bringing in only $45 dollars the night before
by servicing two taxi drivers
and a college kid who braved an equally cold Friday night
for some quick companionship.

The Capitol dome illuminated
in the background
by the cloudy moonlight,
the music of a Capitol Hill Christmas party
too far away to hear,
while congressman and senators
clink glasses and celebrate the Christmas recess
under the Rotunda,
and the feeling that all is well tonight
in the District of Columbia
in this time of great chaos.

13 February 2009

The condom broke on Father's Day

Life

Morning Rain

The water, hot as rain
during an August thunderstorm
in Arizona,
doesn't always clean
the dirt away.
Deep in contemplation,
the morning shower
sheds the dead skin
scabbed over,
releasing pain from a soul
in the quiet of that room
now thick with fog,
filled with feelings,
always silent,
of all I have wasted and lost,
but sometimes gained.
A life filled with regret
and frustration like so many others,
thought to be a success
by those who pay me compliments.
Yet alone with my soul,
the water washes over me,
and I think of all that should be,
but isn't, and wonder is it fair,
no mansion on the hill to call my own,
no beauty queen beside me or
a stable of polo ponies
to play with on a Thursday afternoon.
Wet and weak,
from somber thought,
a quick toweling,
and into my suit with
shirt starched stiff,
a silk tie
in a Windsor knot
and folded white pocket square,
my daily uniform,
proving those words
given to me as a boy
to be true,
a well tailored suit
hides a lot of scars.

25 February 2009

VICTORY

Three cold winters
I've sat by a wood burning stove
and watched my love for you
dance in the flames and disappear
up the flue into a crisp blue sky
filled with the scent of hickory and oak.

You, incarcerated down in Framingham
for the death of our neighbor, your second cousin,
killed off that curve on Dairy Road
that caught the Wilson twins this summer.

The beer and shots to celebrate the victory,
our amazing come from behind victory,
by a single point, five seconds left on the clock,
in overtime
and the bar filled with raucous jubilation
of friends and neighbors unified in our joyous victory
as the beer flowed free.

Toasts made to every player on our team
as we celebrated our blessed victory.

Our victory.

A hollow victory.

A god damn hollow victory splashed across
the morning paper 21- 20.

A victory that destroyed the lives of so many in this town.
You, sent away. Your cousin, in a cold grave.
Everyone here vocal with their opinion on justice.
Justice void of victory as the judge,
a quiet man I once danced with at a cousin's wedding,
sentenced you to four years for vehicular manslaughter,
saying the law is plain in its prescription for man's deeds
when there are only losers.

I sit by this fire and count the things
that had to happen to win that game
by a single point in overtime,
any one out of perfect order
would have had you here
with me for these
three cold winters.

7 August 09

Marrying

Jesus

A Latina, young and beautiful,
with black ringlets to my waist
topped with the rhinestone veil my sister wore
and the communion dress
of satin and lace made by my
Grandma just for me.
I was a bride for Jesus
as they paraded us through the streets
past St. Cecelia's celebrating our purity,
in a neighborhood, anything but pure,
with junkies and dealers on the street
thick as cockroaches in the kitchen
on a Monday morning,
always there.

Ten years later, not as cute,
with my tongue pierced
and my short black hair,
I can still turn heads.
Thick.
With meat on my bones that
shows my curves,
a real woman who always
earns the attention of the black men
with their attitude of invincibility.
They give me a smile
and a line and tell me they can rock my world
and make me see Jesus,
but I just smile and walk on by.
I've been there before,
fourteen,
not a girl, but still not a woman,
riding a man twice my age who painted me with compliments

until he got me into bed,
then taunted me with words of anger,
as he raped me,
telling me to call him daddy,
while he pulled my hair
like the reins of a pony,
no words of love or passion,
but I didn't cry, or tell a soul.
Me, just another claim of victory,
won by his slick lies,
and no I didn't see Jesus,
though I prayed the Hail Mary.

Now, far wiser, I know men and their
attitude and come on lines,
but I only bite when I want to, no longer
needing a man to build me up or pay my way.
I don't have much, but it's all mine.
I see the world as it really is.

Saturday night I take the train
with my girlfriends into Manhattan,
dressed in my new pressed blue jeans,
tight enough to show my curves,
and a knock-off Dolce and Gabana top
I bought in Chinatown.
I'm no J-Lo, but I'm still fine
and damn, I dance better than her.

Early Sunday morning, after the clubs close,
we stop at the all-night diner and eat waffles
and laugh about the men we met with silk suits
and gold chains and their polished silky
see through lines that only my best friend Rosalina buys,
going home with some new Latin lover each time.

My girlfriends tease me, pregnant without a man,
knowing, not telling, who the father is, 'cuz I don't need
a man to make me, me.
Baby, I'm Maria Rosa Gonzalez
and I've already worn that wedding dress
when I was eight and
I got a tattoo of Jesus on my back to prove I was once a bride.
I get all I need cleaning apartments in the city,
three girls and my cousin working for me.
No longer a child, I'm a business woman, moving into a nice
apartment in the Bronx, all my own, in the springtime.

10 February 2009

The oar glides through the water swollen with colors,
escaped from a kaleidoscope - blues and greens and reds,
churned at the surface releasing frustrations from a woman
lost from God, yielding hope with each paddle.

Her evening shower, Sunday before a date with that new guy
with the great hair and the crappy car and reservations
to her favorite Thai place down on Sullivan Street
her only concern, until the moment she wrapped that towel
still warm around her and noticed such a little lump,
hard as dime.

Instant fear remembering her mother's mastectomy at thirty three,
dead by forty one. The endless pills and treatments that caused her
to disappear drop by drop by drop as the poison took no prisoners.

Sunday's date blurred. He rattled on about passing the bar exam,
and college loans and the number of Starbucks in China.
Her only concern, the doctor's appointment (voice mailed) for Monday afternoon.

The oar dipped in the water, churns the colors of the office towers reflected over the
river bank blurring the kaleidoscopic water as she worries about the biopsy results
due tomorrow. Alone on the water, she searches deep to retrieve courage and wait.

1 July 2009

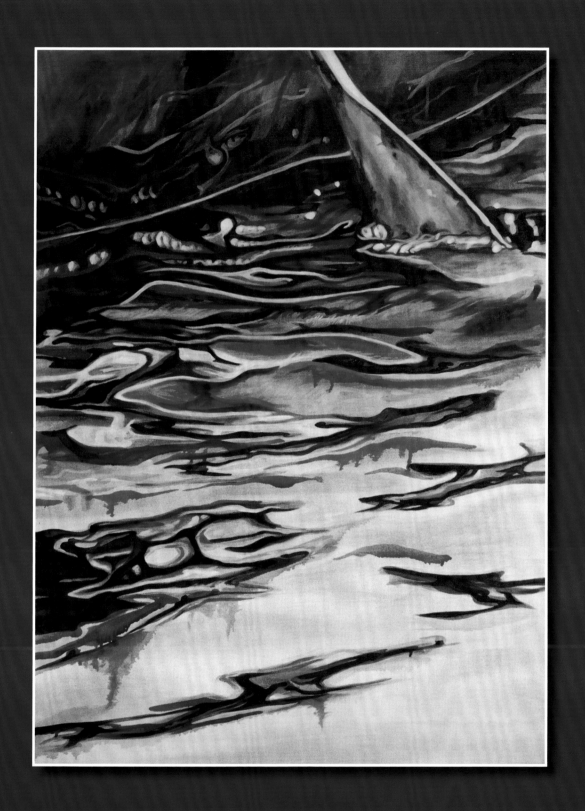

Dancing with Betty Grable

The night he danced with Betty Grable
at the Hollywood Canteen,
he bragged to his buddies at the base
about his foxtrot with the pinup queen,
and told his dad in a postcard written in Greek,
pausing as he wrote her name slowly in English,
mouthing each letter, savoring the remembrance,
and her peck on his check.

He remembered that dance
as his B-29 fell from the sky,
corkscrewing like a meteor in the darkness
in that German night,
its wings clipped off at odd angles,
fire all about,
horrified with the realization
that he'd been the only one to make it out.
As the plane exploded beneath him,
he sobbed as the ground slowly advanced
floating on an angel's sail in a coal black sky
filled with a billion dots of star light,
thinking back to how he hated jump school.
He thought himself a fool,
that she would be one of his last memories,
after all, it was just one dance.

He was rescued from that German wheat field,
and in an hospital in the English countryside
told them all about his buddies on the Marcie Lee,
the bomber named for the mother of her captain.
After weeks of bed rest,
he'd wheel himself into base canteen
where he'd tell the story
of the dance with that pinup queen.
A year later, back in Ohio, he took a bride.
On his wedding day,
he dreamt of holding that movie star
as he held his wife;
the band playing that song
he once shared with her,
as he now started a new life.

He got a job. He bought a house.
He had three sons.

But the nightmare of seeing his buddies die,
in that midnight sky
left him filled with pain that only with cheap whiskey
or Pikesville rye could chase away.
It was never just a glass,
nor was the pain just a memory.
The sight of seeing that explosion
and the instant death of his nine best friends
so vivid,
he could feel the heat in his sleep
as the vibration tore through his soul
and the pain withered his desire
to be a husband and father.
Pain burning so deep it required alcohol
to numb his life to tolerable.

Like so many,
he found himself living for the bottle;
when he was wasn't drunk,
he was mopping the floor
of the gymnasium at the high school
or working midnights stocking shelves
in the town's grocery store.
He'd do odd jobs to pay the rent
on his one bedroom bungalow,
two miles past town, off the gravel road,
near where the respectable families
discarded their junk.

A man all alone with no future and a haunted past.
His children had forgotten him,
after he made his mistress the bottle.
He'd rattle on for hours about nothing
until the world chased him away.
But he held tight to the memory
of dancing with Betty Grable,
and would spend the day telling anyone
who would listen to the story of the dance.
Most just thought him crazy,
the very thought insane. After all,
why would a movie star ever spend a night dancing
with a man like him?

30 March 2009

RICE

There it lay a single grain,
off the plate on the floor
next to a pea,
green as a wax crayon,
freed last night after Zeus,
the family cockapoo, decided to seize the opportunity
presented by the ring of the doorbell,
the delivery man returning with change for a hundred,
the caller forgetting that they didn't accept credit cards
for the lo mein, and their famous
house fried rice
and the Peking duck,
with crispy skin, bronzed and perfect as always,
the center flesh as succulent
as grandma's cream corn
on a cold winter's evening.
It was a fine specimen, once brown,
then white,
now brown again from Kikkoman and spice,
resting under the table
until the pregnant
Maria Rosa, the Puerto Rican housekeeper
with the purple finger nails
and a tattoo of Jesus,
comes to clean the apartment
at 10:30.

5 February 2009

TRUTHS

The sun always shines
after a hurricane, always.

A mother's love is the most
powerful force on earth.

New love can hide flaws
bright as the high noon
August sun.

The shortest distance to
the ice cream shop is
on a father's shoulders.

The bonds of friendship are like kisses on the wind,
always there.

There is no sound sadder
than a mother's wail
for a lost child.

Memories of my failures
burn deep in the silent night
and then I remember
the sun always shines after a hurricane,
always.

POKERFACE

Four cards left,
all the aces spent.
She pulled a three
and smiled as
her daddy said, "Go fish."

EUROPE IN THE DARKNESS

All alone
among the blank faces of a crowded train car.
Their tongue is not yours,
and though you know a few trite phases,
you sit between the obese woman with the soiled dress
and the salami breath
and the little man with a wrinkled face
and a
huge cigar,
and stare at the finger smeared windows
and wonder.

Time moves with a blur
as you trek
across Europe
in darkness.

Written in route to Venice
June 26, 1984

DRIVING TO THE LAND OF DREAMS

On the drive to his dreams,
he felt uneasy and began
to choke. His eyes watered
and he asked the driver
to pull over so he could
compose himself.

He wanted nothing more than
to be a star on the Silver Screen
and speak memorable words to
beautiful leading ladies. He had
the looks, the talent, the gift.

In the darkness to the airport,
they saw a falling star
and together they smiled.
"Don't say it. I already did,"
he told the driver as he choked
up the words.

They drove in silence one
praying, the other knowing,
that the actor would make it
in the land of dreams.

At the airport, the two
men embraced and said
their pleasantries as the
porter whisked away his baggage
and with it the actor began the journey
to be the man he had always
intended to be.

1 February 2009

BISCUITS AND BUTTERMILK

Biscuits in the oven and scrapple on the stove,
the aroma of frying pork heavy in the air
on a cool spring morning.
Gentle hands, thin and frail
with veins that telegraph
the victories and sorrows of eighty years
heaping three dozen scrambled eggs from
the cast iron pan into a casserole dish
to be covered with handfuls of sharp cheddar
bought last week from Mr. Smith's General Store,
baked until it oozes over the eggs, piping hot,
flowing down the dish like lava down Vesuvius.
This meal served daily with pitchers of fresh buttermilk
and coffee, strong and hot,
to a dozen boarders or passersby,
down on their luck, without a real job
or future to hold on to.
Breakfast served here each morning at seven to honor
men in need of a meal, made with love,
for men used to working hard, in a mill or factory
or ditch laying sewer pipe by the mile.
They come to Miss Bertha's house,
the widow of the preacher,
a believer in the Gospel,
who performs miracles everyday for the men
sent down the long gravel road to her farmhouse.
She never offers a handout – always a strong hand
happy to fix the fence,
or build a shed
or clear a field ripe with melons or beans
or an orchard filled with its three types of apples come late September.
She gives these men
the respect they once had,
transforming them into the proud men they use to be,
before the nation in the midst of this great depression
gripped in fear
closed all the factories down,
and with it
the dignity of a generation.

7 March 2009

MICHIGAN AVENUE

The hurried sky so angry now
about to cry a trillion tears
causes pause to the shoppers on Michigan Avenue
as they search for a taxi, or a doorway, or another blue dress
as the summer storm rolls across Lake Michigan.
The old woman just sits and drinks her tea, hot as steam,
and watches the shoppers scamper,
their bundles branded with store logos,
their day interrupted by the driving rain,
as she stares out of the rained streaked window,
loneliness washing over her,
thinking back to those days she shopped here
with girlfriends and children
and every once in a while her husband,
but that – that was forty years ago,
when a summer rain evoked different feelings,
and her time was too valuable to spend the day
hiding in a diner
all alone
just to watch it rain.

14 June 2009

Mallards

Two ducks,
mallards,
the drake with his iridescent green head
and blue wing markings,
and his mate in shades of brown,
swim in the small pond
with the trickling waterfall,
soothing to the nurses
taking long drags on their cigarettes
as an ambulance delivers
another car crash victim
to Good Samaritan Hospital
Tuesday afternoon.

2 April 2009

DYING ON THE MORNING NEWS

Dying of thirst
on the floor of that giant arena
surrounded by water after the levy broke,
flooding New Orleans with the
brackish sea from Pontchartrain,
as the newscaster becomes the story,
crying out in anger at the frustration
of seeing the elderly man
evacuated from a local hospital
dying before him,
while dark skinned black men by the dozen,
like refugees from Angola,
wave white T-shirts
like flags of surrender
from a highway overpass
in this flooded city,
the great playground for America,
known for filet gumbo and Mardi Gras
and drunk women flashing their tits
before a crowd of thousands,
begging for worthless plastic beads,
made in China, thrown by
men holding cups filled with Hurricanes,
the local elixir that gives local color and pleasure
to this genteel southern city
always inebriated or in pain
awaiting
another hurricane
coming
across the Gulf of Mexico.

1 March 2008

FEEDING CHICKENS

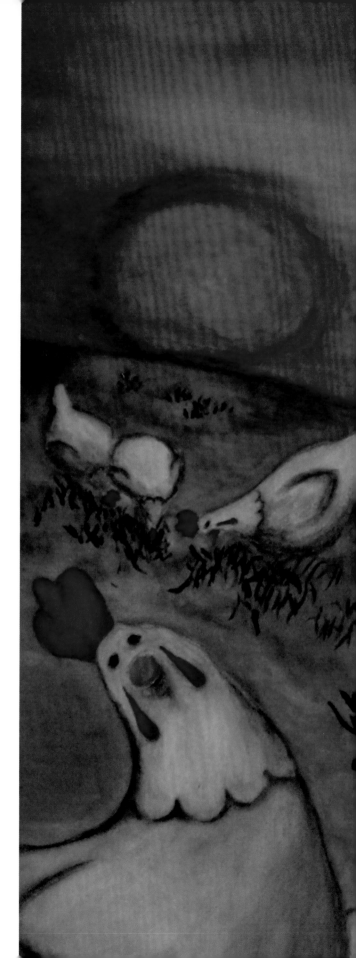

So many dreams
contained within a handful of corn
spread under a pink sunrise
to white chickens
walking on dewy grass
in the fresh air of the country
by the man released from his
Brooks Brothers suit.

6 April 2009

THE DAY FIDEL DIED

Three strong cups of Cuban coffee
start the celebration
that keeps little Havana up past sunrise.
The bars that line the palm studded boulevard
alive as a Chinese dragon.
The beat loud and fast as locals,
children of refugees
from that island nation,
who had love for their seized country
seared into their souls since conception,
dance,
in a conga,
their arms over their heads,
sweat covers their bodies
as they glisten in jubilation under the street lights.
While Mr. Alenjandro,
a gray haired professor
of Cuban literature, now in exile,
sits on his balcony
with his wife, Juliana,
and drinks mojitos.
He puffs on his cigar
and
savors this moment
that two generations prayed for
as church bells across Miami
toll for an hour
at sunrise.   25 March 2009

EVIL

The face of evil is pretty ordinary,
a father with a law degree,
a mother stocking shelves at the local supermarket,
the postman who always gives a treat
to the dogs on his route,
and then one day,
a lightening bolt explodes in their brain
and evil washes over them,
ordering them to kill
those whom they loved the most,
or a total stranger washing his car
in a driveway.

There is never a reason when evil calls,
unless you believe that God
hasn't given free will to man.
Evil - we fear the randomness of it all,
living with the illusion that we are safest in our home,
or a country church on a rainy Sunday morning,
until we see the television crews
standing outside the yellow police tape
as the bleached blonde reporter,
a year out of college,
stands with her microphone
and recants the grizzly details
knowing all too well,
if it bleeds, it leads.

The face of evil is pretty ordinary.
In fact, we've seen it a thousand times,
a father with a law degree,
a mother stocking shelves at the local supermarket,
the postman who always gives a treat
to the dogs on his route,
until the shocking reality of the six o'clock news
proves that the seeds of evil dwell deep within all us
waiting for that trigger allowing it to wash our humanity away.

11 May 2009

OBAMA

Learning. Thinking. Reading.
Growing. Debating. Persuading.
Knowing that he could leave
the concrete jungle
of hatred and ignorance
is what gave him
the inspiration
to rise
above
his
circumstances
such
a long time ago
to attempt to
govern a nation
filled with such pain
and confusion
now infused with the burning desire
for a leader
unlike all the others
to save us from ourselves.

11 February 2009

Little Italy, 1964

There are no secrets here, only lies,
told by our grandmothers
as they wash their steps each morning at ten.
Spreading the news about their children
and their children's friends,
the law degrees, the pregnancies, the jobs won and lost
uptown and down on the pier by their husbands
and now their sons,
unloading steamships arriving from distant lands.
They tell of the weddings and the money spent,
gossiping about Angelo's daughter,
such a beautiful bride and how she didn't show
in the gown made by Mrs. Pettrillio.
Mrs. Romano, the insomniac mayor of our neighborhood,
says she remembers the little whore
walking down the street before sunrise
carrying her shoes, her blouse hanging out,
having done the deed of the devil.
She makes the sign of the cross and spits.
"I knew that she was going to get knocked up
by some good time Charlie."
But the women just smile and start talking
about the murder of a police officer,
from a family who moved from here when he was three.
No suspects the radio says,
but they all think it was the mafia or a jealous husband
or a black boy he must have arrested weeks ago.
The topics wander until it comes to food and they talk
about the braised eggplant made last night for dinner or
the lamb shank roasted in wine and garlic
until it fell from the bone,
and Mrs. Cavalera gives the women her recipe
for her veal that the visiting priest
referenced in his sermon last Sunday.
On cue, as the restaurateurs begin setting up their tables
on the sidewalk preparing for the lunch crowd,
the ladies put down their brushes and empty their pails
until tomorrow, when they shall wash the gossip
down with vinegar once more.

6 April 2009

The Land of Pleasant Living

The kitchen table covered with the Baltimore Sunday Sun,
spread out and overlapped two sheets thick, protecting the wood
from salt and spice and pointed orange shells piled higher than beer cans.
Pitchers of iced tea and a case of iced cold ones sit on the counter next to plates of Silver Queen,
hot and buttery, and baskets of rough cut french fries,
and freshly battered onion rings, thick and greasy and too hot to touch.
A bushel of extra large,
their shells coated in a thick crust of salt and Old Bay,
form the center piece of the table.
Eager hands reach into the pile pulling out the biggest crab
as soon as they are poured from the pot.
The air explodes with conversation of the O's
and greats like the Robinsons, Ripken, Murray, Dempsey and Weaver
as WBAL plays in the background from the neighbor's front room.
Evening fades to night,
misquotes feast on the feasting
while children keep count as the pile of crabs forms an even larger pile of shells,
amazed that Grandma Gert holds her own with Uncle Bud,
at a dozen each, as their bedtime approaches.

The morning trash piled high,
filled with husk of corn and shell of crab
and the rattle of a case of cheap beer,
a proud a monument
found throughout Baltimore neighborhoods
of a Friday payday
and a Sunday celebration of life
in the land of pleasant living.

4 November 2008

142

My Exodus

My momma whispered,
"never more shall you live here,
the son of a beggar,
a boy dressed in rags and hand-me-downs
from those no richer than you.
Go and seek your fortune across the ocean.
Never say the name of this place of misery and misfortune,
filled with generations Jews and widows,
all starving as we light the candles come Shabbat.
Make your passage – as steerage or stowaway,
but find yourself facing that lady in the harbor before winter.
Kiss your momma's tears before you walk across the broken cobblestones
to make your exodus."

Eighty years later, my fortune made in paving roads across America,
my wealth, now public record, brings me accolades and bequests
from Jew and Gentile and the name I gave myself at Ellis Island,
Gomel, after that town filled with misery, all its Jews murdered by the Nazis,
is now repeated with pride
as I meet with the senators and bankers,
or my tailor on a Monday morning to be fitted for new silk suits,
my waist growing too fat from decadent desserts and no exercise.

When I die, I ask that you lay broken cobblestones on my grave
to celebrate this country, honor a whisperer, and mark my exodus.

.

28 June 2009

Jamaica Last Chance Pawn

He lost her love
at the Jamaica Last Chance Pawn
down on Benthurst Avenue,
across from where
they met thirty years before,
when the number 19 trolley
still ran past there to the shore.
The place was still a dump,
in seventy years
it hadn't changed at all,
still filled with other's people's junk
hocked to pay the rent
or buy groceries
or new tires for the car.
Some of it was stolen,
but you would never know.
No one asks questions
and no one every tells
when they hock their stuff
with the pawnbroker
old Mr. Abraham
with the deep blue eyes,
a story buried deep inside.
And so it was my father,
who borrowed against her
wedding rings,
just enough for payroll
until the cash
came rolling in
and he could get them back
and return them to his bride.

A sacred bond was broken
on that dreadful Friday
when they sold
my mother's rings
and sold her soul as well
for just a couple dollars
at the Jamaica Last Chance Pawn
down on Benthurst Avenue,
across from where
they met thirty years before,
but the number 19 trolley
doesn't run out there any more.

7 February 2009

Sunday Dinner at the Hotel des Jardin

The sundae, cold and beautiful,
to the two year old having the tantrum,
her grandmother extends a spoonful,
commanding silence and a smile,
like Moses parting the Red Sea.
The restaurant noise quieted with her calming,
as the diners look to her table with a reassuring smile,
while the waiter, in his crisp tuxedo,
picks up a dropped napkin from the floor.

20 March 2009

Cupcakes on the Table

The cupcake on the table,
a masterpiece of creation
decorated by his three year
old daughter home sick from
pre-school with a broken foot
earned by beating her four year old
brother down from the second floor
steps by jumping all the way
and landing hard on the freshly
polished oak floor.
The cupcake her favorite, lemon
with orange butter cream icing
so rich it makes her pucker,
the zest of a tangerine,
the secret ingredient,
never a navel, blood
or clementine. The icing
thick as biscuit batter with
specks of vanilla bean peaking throughout.
The icing heaped over the top
of an oversized cupcake
he made in her mother's muffin tin,
normally reserved for muffins - blueberry,
cranberry or peach, served on lazy Sundays
when they have out-of-town visitors
on their way to New Jersey to visit
her mother's brother and her
older cousin, who lost his mother
in the World Trade Tower.
The cupcake, actually a dozen of them,
sit on the table cooling off
before her father covers them
in orange zest,
grated with the shinny mandolin
he bought at Crate and Barrel
the last time he went to Bethesda.

22 February 2009

Loving you always

Dear mom and dad

April Fool

The girl
sat there looking out to the freeway,
tears streaming down her cheek,
in this cheap hotel room,
regretting the journey with her boyfriend,
two years older than her father,
twenty dollars in her pocket,
a thousand miles from home,
wadded tissues tossed carelessly
on the floor,
her cell phone out of juice,
from crying to her mother
after her boyfriend passed out
from drinking a bottle of tequila,
before throwing his car keys at her,
hitting her cheek,
making it bleed
before the ring of keys
landed hard after bouncing off the motel the door,
the TV playing a black and white
rerun of the Andy Griffith Show,
the volume turned off,
the girl in contemplation,
wanting to tell her Daddy,
she wanted his forgiveness
and return home to her bedroom,
with its dated pink wallpaper,
and their small, fifty year old rancher
in the working class suburbs of Chicago,
and simply to be his little girl again,
like she had been for the last 18 years,
until the day she ran away with the neighbor,
the father of her best friend,
driving his classic Dodge Charger,
on their way to California,
when they stopped at this no frills
hotel with a third floor window
facing the freeway
on a crisp sunny day
on the first of April.

22 February 2009

Spring

Spring is the season celebrated by old men and poets,
each thankful for new life after the darkness of winter.

It is the time when children shed those dreaded winter coats
and mothers fret about the extra ten pounds gained after the winter solstice.

It is the season that farmers, gamblers all, bet on a bumper crop
while pouring seeds into the tilted ground, still cold.

It is the time when grave diggers working for small cemeteries
in the Dakotas and Canada's Northwest Territory
can again tend to unfinished business and break the ground,
once hard as granite, to lay to rest
all those who didn't win another spring.

Spring is the season celebrated by those models in
The New York Times dressed only in ribbons of silk,
the sun bathing their perfect skin,
while they peddle famous French perfume,
a hallmark that garden parties and expensive outdoor weddings
will soon be in bloom.

Spring is the only season that features a symphony found in every wood
and pond and patch of grass big enough to sprout a tulip or daffodil.

Spring is what man would have made if it wasn't already a gift from God.

4 June 2009

Pool Boys

Two fat girls
lounge
near a turquoise pool
framed by a hundred
sticks
sheathed in
pocket squares
of pink neon
striped and patterned
primary colors
and a single leopard print.
The fabric,
strategically arranged
to keep those muscular boys
on the high dive
erect
before
they twist into three somersaults
and unfold like a
gannet
diving
into
a school of shad.
The boys
singularly
surface
to praise and adulation
from the bronzed women
who spend their summer
on pool chairs,
their backs slathered in
lotion,
their bikini straps
untied
as
a radio plays
Hey Jude.

13 July 2009

Paralyzed in 1992, Christopher has taught himself to paint by holding paintbrush in his mouth.

TANNEBAUM

The crickets, gone with the frost,
now a permanent visitor each morning
to these woods that make my footprints
crackle over the leaves brown and hard
with their beauty long gone.
They will turn to earth, rich and black, by spring,
just in time for the wildflowers
that come through this wood by the first of April,
and vanish by the time the dogwood blooms.
But spring is still a distant memory,
a reward for suffering through the endless
snowfalls yet to come and hauling the cords of wood
I cut from here each autumn to heat my home,
perched at the entrance to this sacred place.

My journey this morning is to find that magnificent pine
I saw last summer while searching for our collie dog
that vanished like the wildflowers.
Twenty acres of woods separate our property
from the state hospital filled with patients
on sabbatical from reality.
Harmless, most, and easy to tell
with their orange canvass sneakers
and their eyes that stare out beyond the horizon,
while a conversation unfolds within their head.
Their eyes always too intense to see life
around them as they fight the demons not medicated away.

The morning landscape hard, dappled with the green of the
holly and pine, but mainly gray from hardwoods
of oak and maple,
their branches void of camouflage,
revealing a cardinal's nest
and the scars of a woodpecker and, high above me,
floating like a castle in the morning sky,
the massive home to generations of paper wasps.

Through puffs of breath,
the coldness numbing my cheeks,
I see my tree, that pine, as magnificent as I remember.
Twelve feet tall with every branch full and round,
the perfect specimen
that my little ones will soon decorate with Christmas tinsel
and paper chains and topped with a blessed angel
with hand painted eyes and wings of blown glass;
a family treasure brought from Germany
a hundred years ago,
that I bought this summer at an estate sale for a dollar.

I am startled by the stranger sitting
on a stump next to my tree.
A big man wearing blue bib overalls
and those strange orange sneakers.
His face is solemn, without a smile,
but with lines that tell he's lived a life harder
than mine, and his hands,
double the size of my hands are hard
with calluses and scars.

I notice that the knuckle of his little finger is missing,
as he extends his hand to shake,
calling me friend and inviting me to sit down
and talk with him.

He points to a stump,
as I place my ax beneath my feet,
my work boots firmly resting
on the handle of hickory and I tell him my name.
Again, he calls me friend and asks why I am walking
these woods this morning,
unaware that Christmas is in five days.
I give him my reason;
he shrugs as he says it is indeed a beautiful tree,
like the kind he remembers cutting
with his father fifty years ago
off their land in Washington County.

I ask why he is in that hospital
and he tells me that he killed his brother
with an ax, much like mine, during an argument over
inheriting the family farm.
The judge has sent him here to mourn
and regret his deed,
until the he's no longer crazy and can be set free.

He smiles and tells me to get to work taking the tree,
but my ax is frozen beneeth my feet.
I am now too afraid to move.
He laughs and tells me to cut the tree; he's no harm
and anyway it's time for his breakfast.
Today, they're serving pancakes with blueberry syrup,
and he can't be late.
He hugs my shoulder as a friend
and, without words or smile, leaves the woods
down a path I've walked a dozen times before.
I sit upon my stump and think awhile,
blowing puffs of breath over my gloves,
my heart still racing as I stare at that magnificent pine
and ponder,
thinking about the brother I haven't spoken to
in twenty years
and about the invitation I'll now make
to Christmas dinner
when I return with this magnificent tannebaum.

11 April 2009

Chesapeake Bay Mourning

The whirring of the wind over the canvas
as the hull glides through the waters of the Chesapeake
on a blustery Wednesday afternoon adds life to my spirit.
High above me is the underbelly of the great dual-spanned bridge
named in honor of William Preston Lane, Jr.,
but nobody knows that as they pull sweet rock fish from its shadow.
I crane my neck, staring up past the sea gulls to the bridge deck
and remember fishing under this bridge as a small boy,
the year that five bridge painters fell to their deaths one summer.
I remember saying an Our Father for them beneath my breath
as my father broke open a beer
and handing it to his fishing buddy joked
about it be being a quick death on the water.

Off the channel, moored in the bay, rest eight monstrous cargo ships,
awaiting orders after unloading autos and sugar and wind turbines made in Spain
at the Port of Baltimore, their uneasy stillness a sign of our current recession.
Fifty years ago this channel was packed with ore freighters heading to the Bethlehem Steel plant
at Sparrows Point. Then, The Point use to employ thirty thousand men making steel,
the back bone for America, at her water's edge,
but no more.

As a boy, the bay used to scare me.
It was the size of an ocean, overwhelming to a ten year old
struggling to pull crab traps,
filled with angry blue crabs,
lured by chicken necks tied tight,
from the rolling gray water.
I see this bay once teaming with life now dying,
like the fate of a favorite aunt who suffered through too many cigarettes
while frying collards in fatback.

Come dawn, the gulls dance through the air celebrating a recent fish kill,
as a school of blue gills suffocated by an algae bloom float on the surface.
Their corpses, a silvery bounty honored
with the screams and hollers as loud as frat house brothers on spring break.
I feel the wind stinging my face as we glide through the water,
the roar of the sails bringing meaning to life
as the sun sets over the Bay Bridge and darkness fills the moonless night.

21 May 2009

Vacationland in Darkness

The morning, not black,
but gray like smoke over a mountain top
with a glint of pink near the horizon
where the condo buildings
touch the bay.
And the water under the boardwalk laps gently against the pier,
not fierce like it did last August with the hurricane
that took down the Ferris wheel,
with its multi-colored fluorescent lights
that illuminate throughout the night
bringing reverence to the spot where many shared a vacationland kiss.
The hurricane, a category three,
caused so much pain to vacationers
forcing them away from their yearly paradise with its destruction of this town.

No, this morning, the wind is quiet,
still sleeping like the kites and surfboards resting in the back of the family SUV,
ready to be the focus of this town's attention,
but not now.

The beach,
the heart of this place, is clean again of candy wrappers and footprints.
And the sound of carnival barkers,
crying babies and laughter has been replaced with the footsteps of a morning jogger,
running in the darkness,
a black silhouette fading towards the morning light.
The smell of french fries and funnel cakes and pizza by the slice
has been purified by the warm salt air,
comforting on the cheek.

The forms of buildings beyond the blackened boardwalk will soon come to life
with their flashing signs and needless merchandise,
a treasure for those left home, waving in the summer breeze.
Soon the boardwalk will be filled with the sounds of the penny arcade
with its pinball machines and video games, and families playing skee ball
and the rifle range with its moving targets
plunked down with each bull's eye.

Laughter and squeals of glee coming from children on the bumper cars,
filled with happiness of being here on their summer vacation, will soon be replaced
only by the deafening sounds of silence as teenage lovers,
young, quiet and scared, share a first kiss on the rebuilt Ferris wheel,
come twilight.

4 March 2009

A CHANCE MEETING

You were so beautiful to me
I forgot to tell you my name,
as I quickly reached for your business card,
my wife tugging at my sleeve.
I said you looked familiar,
like a friend of mine from long ago.
Then you told us you were from Rochester
and I began to wonder, though I already knew.
As you described your mother
and the restaurant she owned,
a gift from her father when her mother died.
I knew then you were my daughter.
But with my wife next to me,
I couldn't say a word,
or give you the kiss and hug that I needed to
or tell you that I was sorry
for abandoning your mother,
whom I never stopped loving
once she told me of her blessing
on the day I turned thirty.
She cursed me with that news
just a month past my wedding day,
thirty three years ago.
Our story was so complicated;
with my father making me marry the
woman to my right for the sake
of family appearances
and your grandmother
keeping your mother
from marrying me
because I wasn't a Jew,
but that was such a long time ago.
I asked what your father did?
You said you did not know.
You never met the man.
When I asked you if you
wanted to know your dad?
You smiled and said,
"You know sir, I really don't know."
That's when I smiled and said,
"Good morning, Virginia.
I'm glad to meet you.
My name is Harry Crain."

18 February 2009

PAIN

Dripping

Enveloping
Life

Until
its agonizing twisted existence is your existence.

Life is removed from its victim by the ounce until the strong athletic form is reduced
to a weak whimpering mass in search of relief from a pill, a patch, a bottle.

The night grows long.

The hours fade slowly, too slowly.

Tired and in agony,

I will pray for sleep to overtake me,

but it never does.

Exhaustion,

like crucifixion,

allows rest to slowly fill me

until morning.

Always knowing that the pain is guarding my existence,

I do not slumber,

I do not rest.

I am merely passing time, the pain playing me for a couple of precious hours until

at last it pretends to award me victory,

only to smack me down like a punk.

30 May 2005

AUTUMN LEAVES

colors blur
in the afternoon darkness
of a warm November
fading from intensity
as
powder blush
crumbles
into a cold
cruel death
their very
existence snuffed from within.

18 November 1987

FRIDAY NIGHT AT THE EAST GATE MALL

They come there as a rite of passage
to celebrate with their friends
over burgers and shakes,
sharing laughter and young love.
School girls flirting with their bad boy boyfriends,
the ones their mothers would never
approve of with baggy pants
and hip hop T-shirts and their Yankee
baseball caps flipped back to show of their
diamond earring.
The girls feel like women when
those boys, soon to be marines,
sporting fierce tattoos over their muscular biceps,
hold them tight and tell them that they're beautiful
in front of the Taco Bell.

The cheerleaders and the loners both congregate
at the food court with the smell of Cinnabon
heavy in the air and the Asian woman handing out
samples of bourbon chicken to all the passersby;
the line at the Chick-fil-A twenty deep with
mothers getting dinner for their babies
and sales clerks taking
their evening break.

The women from three counties still come by to
search for new shoes for their cousin's wedding
or a dreaded bathing suit for that luxury cruise
they saved for two years to celebrate their twentieth anniversary.
The men come too, shopping at Sears
to purchase band saw blades, new coveralls or something for the
car, but the stores aren't so busy anymore.
This town has been hit hard with the failing economy;
so many fathers out of work since they closed
the plant and the planners in Washington
re-routed the interstate to bypass our county.
The retailers trying to sell their wares any way they can
with their 40% off sales and banners in their windows
celebrating spending, sexy girls pictured on them.
Still the folks around here don't buy,
scared to make a move or spend a buck
on anything they don't really need,
except for the Lotto, a dream of endless wealth, for a buck.

The mall is filled with empty shoppers who
come in droves on Friday night to meet their friends
and forget about their worries
over ice cream at the Dairy Queen
while the teens celebrate a rite of passage
and grow into young adults on
the parking lot until they take the interstate
away from this place finding their future in
another state a couple of months
past graduation day.

22 February 2009

THROUGH THE FROZEN WOOD

A February rain,
cold and painful,
falls on crystallized woods,
branches thick with ice
glisten and creak
while frozen drops of rain
sting my flesh
with the fervor of hornets
vindicating their queen.
Ten thousand stalactites,
like shards of glass,
strain to remain in formation
along each bough and branch,
their weight the final torment
to those oaks,
tired as gravediggers,
and contorted like Chinese acrobats,
that give me pause as I trod beneath a forest
genuflecting to an artic queen.
At last,
I find a patch of ground
soft enough to dig
and suitable as the final resting place for
Luke, a jet black Labrador,
frozen by death
after losing his battle with a brown bear
he startled
on our walk
through these woods
this morning.

10 July 2009

Writer's Block

When will the well run dry?
And once again
I lie in bed waiting
for the words to come
like cactus flowers
after a driving desert rain.

27 January 2009